Phil Shaw is a 31 year old hi-stakes poker player, writer and journalist from London, England. He specializes in high stakes online play including $5/10-$25/50 no limit hold'em cash games, $30/60-$200/400 fixed limit games, $200-$2,000 sitngos and hi-stakes online tournaments. He discovered online poker whilst trying (and failing) to watch the Bruce Willis film *The Jackal* on television in April 2002 and opened his first poker account in that name whilst still a student. He has been known by variations of it ever since, including "Jackal69" on PokerStars and "Jackal78" on Full Tilt Poker.

He graduated from Keble College, Oxford University in 2003 with a BA in English Language and Literature and currently writes for a variety of publications on poker including *Inside Poker* and *Poker Player* by Dennis Publishing, and is a Guest Pro on poker video instructional site *CardRunners* alongside players like Brian Townsend and Taylor Caby, specializing in sitngo and mixed game tuition. He is also the author of *Secrets of Sitngos*, released by D & B Publishing in 2007, which has become the definitive text on the subject. His largest single win to date is $76,000 in an online multi-table tournament.

Poker books from D&B

Secrets of Professional Poker, volume 1
by Rolf Slotboom
978-1-904468-40-0, 256pp, $24.95 / £14.99

Advanced Limit-Hold'em Strategy
by Barry Tanenbaum
978-1-904468-36-3, 256pp, $24.95 / £14.99

Secrets of Sit'n'gos
by Phil Shaw
978-1-904468-43-1, 224pp, $24.95 / £14.99

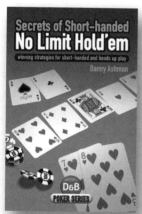

Secrets of Short-handed No Limit Hold'em
by Danny Ashman
978-1-904468-41-7, 208pp, $24.95 / £14.99

How Good is Your Pot-Limit Omaha?
by Stewart Reuben
978-1-904468-07-3, 192pp, $19.95 / £12.99

Secrets of Short-handed Pot-Limit Omaha
by Rolf Slotboom and Rob Hollink
978-1-904468-44-8, 336pp, $27.50 / £15.99

Professional Middle-Limit Hold'em
by Tristan Steiger
978-1-904468-47-9, 336pp, $25.95 / £15.99

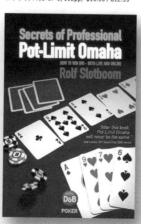

Secrets of Professional Pot-Limit Omaha
by Rolf Slotboom
978-1-904468-30-6, 240pp, $25.95 / £15.99

Limit Hold'em: Winning short-handed strategies
by Terry Borer and Lawrence Mak with Barry Tannenbaum
978-1-904468-37-0, 352pp, $25.95 / £15.99

Secrets of non-standard Sit'n'gos

Phil Shaw

www.dandbpoker.com

First published in 2010 by D & B Publishing

British Library Cataloguing-in-Publication Data

A catalogue record for this book is available from the British Library.

ISBN: 978 1 904468 52 3

All sales enquiries should be directed to D&B Publishing:

Tel: 01273 711443, e-mail: info@dandbpoker.com,

Website: www.dandbpoker.com

Cover design by Horatio Monteverde.

Printed and bound by Versa Press in the US.

Contents

Introduction

About this Book

Since writing *Secrets of Sitngos*[1] many changes have come about in the poker world that have affected these games. New formats have appeared offering a wide variety of choice to sitngo players wanting to try something new; and the standard types of sitngos have become tougher due to an increasing awareness of the correct strategies and computer programs that can assist learning. In response to this poker sites that want to maintain high traffic for sitngo play have introduced reward schemes and leaderboards for high volume and high scoring players.

This book will address many of these changes in the sitngo landscape, most of which have taken place in the last 2-3 years. After reviewing some fundamental sitngo concepts that will apply throughout the book such as the Independent Chip Model (ICM) and short-stack strategy, we will look at fundamental poker concepts such as tournament strategy and hand ranges that it is essential to understand in this new tougher landscape and in the different formats. We will also consider

---

[1] Beginning players should refer back to this book for more complete explanations of many basic sitngo and poker concepts.

some more advanced poker concepts that will aid you if you wish to progress to a very high level. Then we will look at the new formats which have become available in recent years, including Step systems, Double-or-Nothing and Matrix sitngos as well as examining the more conventional alternatives to the nine- or ten-handed game such as Heads-up and Six-max sitngos. Additionally there is information about playing non-hold'em, fixed limit and mixed game sitngos for players looking to expand into other games.

After that we will look at some other advances in the poker world such as new software and poker training sites then move onto other aspects of sitngo play that have become important to professional sitngo players including rakeback, reward programs and leaderboard prizes offered by sites like PokerStars. Here those playing high stakes and high volume can gain hefty compensation from cash bonuses and the Supernova Elite package, and win money in weekly leaderboard competitions. Finally, you will be able to text yourself with quizzes relating to each type of game.

Undoubtedly the sitngo world has changed considerably in the last few years and will continue to evolve, but the introduction of new formats and rewards has ensured that they are still an attractive proposition for new players entering the game, those looking to make serious money and recreational players who like to have fun and gamble. Hopefully all these categories of player will improve significantly from reading the advice that follows.

Chapter One

Review of Fundamental Sitngo Concepts

Secrets of Sitngos offered the reader a comprehensive account of how to approach sitngos, focusing on the full-ring, nine- or ten-player format. In this book we will look at a variety of formats, but it is still important to review some concepts that relate to all sitngo play and that one must understand clearly in order to adapt to specific situations and formats.

We will first look at raise sizes and how they should differ from the early game, when pot raises are permissible, to the late game, when some players choose to min-raise (i.e., double the big blind). Then we will revisit ICM, which is a mechanism that allows us to assign a monetary value to a player's stack of tournament chips, depending on the other players' stacks and the payout structure, and from there determine the best strategies. These will vary radically, depending on whether you are the big, medium or small stack, and whether you are playing a standard format or one like double-or-nothing, in which half the players win double their buy-in and the others get nothing.

Then we will review strategies for short-stack play, when you have 15 big blinds or less. We will consider why moving all-in or folding is often the best strategy in this case, and we will look at situations where you might want to make raises from smaller stacks or bigger shoves, depending on the circumstances. Whatever format of sitngo you are playing, it will be essential to understand the reasoning behind this strategy and how to best implement it.

Raise Sizes

You must decide how to size your opening raises at various points in a sitngo, from early on when you have plenty of chips, to late stages when the blinds are such that you simply move all-in. It is almost universally agreed that you should lower your raise sizes as the blinds rise and the stacks become shorter, but there is no clear consensus on exact sizing.

Some players make a min-raise or small raise early on, and many will min-raise often in the late stages, even from the small blind, whereas more traditional players will open for 3x (three times the big blind) early and bring this down to 2.5x later on. However, opening for more than the pot early on and more than 2.5x late is considered sub-optimal. Choosing a raise size within certain margins is to some extent a matter of playing style. The key is to understand the implications of each style, how your opponents will respond to it and how you should respond to players using each style.

The Early Game

Opening for around 3x is considered optimal in the early game. You are playing relatively deep and do not want other players to come in when you will typically have a strong hand range from early and middle position. You may moderate this by opening to 3.5x or 4x in early position in loose or lower-stakes games to build pots and gain value for your hand range, and making a smaller raise or even min-raise in late position in very tight or aggressive games where you do not need to waste additional chips in an attempt to pick up the blinds.

I don't recommend making smaller raises or min-raising in early or middle position. You are building a pot but not making it expensive enough for drawing hands to make errors by calling. Your prospects spiral downward when ever more players join the cold-calling. With hands you wish to play, you should open with a raise of the appropriate size for your position, or if the game type suits (e.g., loose and passive), consider limping with speculative hands.

Players making small raises in early or middle position allow you to enter many pots cheaply and build pots that give you additional value for your drawing hands. If this occurs while the stacks are still 50 big blinds or deeper, you can call with most suited connectors and suited aces in late position, since you will either have a chance to win a multi-way pot or play the raiser heads-up with position.

You should not defend too lightly out of the blinds, even against min-raises, since you will be playing relatively deep-stacked poker, out of position for the entire hand. But you can call very small raises with all strong, speculative hands like suited aces, suited connectors, small pairs and Broadway hands because it is cheap and the pot is relatively small.

The Middle Game

Your average raise size should come down in the middle game, when the average stacks are around 20-30 big blinds. Few players raise more than 3x at this stage, with some electing for 2.5x or the min-raise. There is room for diversity, but smaller raises are generally recommended with smaller stack sizes (compared to the blinds), because your opponents will be less able to cold-call profitably and there will be fewer multi-way pots.

Determine a raise size that suits your strengths as well as the games you play. Min-raising is likely to see you in more post-flop battles, especially against the big blind, but it can be a good strategy in very tight-aggressive games, whereas 3x will put you in fewer post-flop situations but give shorter-stacked opponents more incentive to re-raise.

Playing against variable raise sizes in the middle game is more awkward because you rarely have the correct odds to cold-call with speculative hands or the right stack size to re-raise all-in. You will need to proceed with caution and consider the merits of each situation. For example, cold-calling a min-raise with 3-3 and a stack of 25 big blinds is often profitable after other callers, but probably not against a single opener, since you will not often stack the raiser even when you hit your set. In the same situation, a hand like A-Js might prefer to flat-call a 3x raise rather than re-raise or fold.

You will have less of a positional disadvantage in the blinds, but even with 20 big blinds, the stacks are still only just the right size to call a 3x raise and check-raise all-in on favorable flops, so you should not defend too lightly. You can still defend a lot of speculative hands against a min-raise, but reduced implied odds make this a marginal play even to a 2.5x raise.

The Late Game

Once most players have less than 20 big blinds, your opening raise should clearly be no greater than 2.5x. Many players have made the min-raise their standard opening, particularly when most players are tight and will either raise or fold in response, so that they can attempt to steal the blinds cheaply and reduce their risk of pot commitment if re-raised.

Min-raising is an excellent strategy in the latter case; there is no reason to risk an extra half-blind against players who raise or fold with similar frequency. However, players are tending to re-raise or defend their blind lighter in the face of min-raises; against them, you should either increase your raise size or be prepared to call all-in re-raises lighter and see more post-flop play.

The big blind is the most likely player to get involved against a min-raise in the late game, since his odds are so good. His stack is ideal for check-raising all-in, and shallow enough to lessen his positional disadvantage. You should call with many speculative hands that can flop big, assuming your opponent has a wide opening range, and especially if he continuation bets too much. Hands such as A-8o, Q-9s, 10-Jo, 10-8s and A-2s are probably unplayable against a raise of even 2.5x, but can be played against a frequent min-raiser, assuming you are not right on the bubble and able to survive until the money, in which case you should probably fold since ICM considerations will be more pressing.

ICM (the Independent Chip Model)

The value of your chips in a sitngo changes over time. Because you are paid based on your finishing position and are unable to cash in your chips during the game, their monetary value changes throughout the event, depending on the number of players remaining, their relative stack sizes and the payout structure.

For example, consider a ten-player $100 sitngo with a standard 50/30/20 payout structure where each player starts with 1,000 chips. Each chip is initially worth ten cents, but in the end, the winning player has all 10,000 and wins the $500 first prize, meaning that each chip is now worth only a nickel. But if a player gets past the bubble with only one chip, then that chip is worth at least $200, as he will finish no worse than third.

The most accurate way to calculate the monetary value of tournament chips at any point in a sitngo is known as the Independent Chip Model (ICM). You can use ICM to determine the relative chances of the players finishing in certain orders and the total real-money equity they would accrue by doing so, given the stacks of all players and the prize structure. The calculations are extremely complex, so most players use programs that perform them instantaneously (see the next chapter).

Let's work through an example to help you understand how ICM functions. Consider the following situation:

Player	Stack Size	Payout Structure	Tournament Equity ($EV)
Player A	4,000	1st $500	?
Player B	3,000	2nd $300	?
Player C	2,000	3rd $200	?
Player D	1,000	4th $0	?

Each of the four remaining players has a different percentage of the chips in play (40/30/20/10). Three prizes are available with a standard 50/30/20 payout structure. From this we must calculate the current real money value of their chips (disregarding factors such as the position of the blinds and the players' relative ability, which are addressed in the chapter "The limitations of ICM"). We can do this according to ICM by calculating each player's chances of finishing in each position and multiplying it by the payout for that place, then summing those values to determine each player's overall expected payout ($EV).

The probability that each player finishes first is directly proportional to the number of chips he has in play. For example, the probability that Player A wins is calculated as P(A finishes 1st) = 4,000/10,000 = 40%. We can start to tabulate our results as follows:

Player	Stack Size	P(1st)	P(2nd)	P(3rd)	P(4th)
Player A	4,000	40%	?	?	?
Player B	3,000	30%	?	?	?
Player C	2,000	20%	?	?	?
Player D	1,000	10%	?	?	?

After this we must calculate the probabilities that the players finish second or third, which is where things get complicated. If we consider Player A first, his chances of finishing second are the sum total of the situations in which one of the other players wins and he beats the remaining two players. There are three possible cases here, and each can be tabulated by multiplying the chance of another player winning the sitngo by the chance that Player A will have of beating the remaining players, the latter measured as the Player A's proportion of the remaining chips. For example, if Player B wins (which we know will happen 30% of the time), there are now 7,000 chips remaining and Player A will have a 4,000/7,000 chance of beating the other two players. Calculating and summing all these values gives us the total probability that Player A will finish second:

P (B wins and A beats C and D) 0.3 * 4,000/7,000 = 0.1714

P (C wins and A beats B and D) 0.2 * 4,000/8,000 = 0.1

P (D wins and A beats B and C) 0.1 * 4,000/9,000 = 0.0444

P (All cases where A finishes 2nd)   = 0.3159 (31.59%)

Calculating the probability that Player A finishes third is even more complicated. We must consider the probability of another player winning outright, and multiply this by the probability that among the three remaining players, another player wins this mini-tournament (to finish second overall) and then Player A beats the remaining player to finish third. There are six ways that this can occur, and they can be considered according to the exact finishing positions of the players from first to fourth. When tabulated this looks like:

P (finishing order of BCAD)	(0.3)(2/7)(4/5)	= 0.0686
P (finishing order of CBAD)	(0.2)(3/8)(4/5)	= 0.06
P (finishing order of BDAC)	(0.3)(1/7)(4/6)	= 0.0286
P (finishing order of DBAC)	(0.1)(3/9)(4/6)	= 0.0222
P (finishing order of CDAB)	(0.2)(1/8)(4/7)	= 0.143
P (finishing order of DCAB)	(0.1)(2/9)(4/7)	= 0.0127
P (All cases where A finishes 3rd)		= 0.2064 (20.64%)

Having calculated the probability of A finishing first to third, it is now easy to calculate his chances of finishing fourth:

P (A finishes 4th) = 1 – P (A finishes 1st-3rd)   = 0.0778 (7.78%)

This gives us a complete set of results for Player A. We can employ the same approach for each player, giving us the following results:

Player	Stack Size	P(1st)	P(2nd)	P(3rd)	P(4th)
Player A	4,000	40%	31.58%	20.64%	7.78%
Player B	3,000	30%	30.83%	26.19%	12.98%
Player C	2,000	20%	24.13%	31.75%	24.12%
Player D	1,000	10%	13.45%	21.43%	55.12%

We can calculate a money value for a player's stack by multiplying his chance of finishing in a certain position by the payout for that position and summing those values (note that fourth place can be excluded as it pays nothing). For Player A this would be as follows:

$EV of Player A   = (0.4)($500) + (0.3158)($300) + (0.2064)($200)

= $336.03

The overall worth of each player's stack from the $1,000 prize pool is as follows:

Player	Stack Size	Payout Structure	Tournament Equity ($EV)
Player A	4,000	1st $500	$336.03
Player B	3,000	2nd $300	$294.87
Player C	2,000	3rd $200	$235.89
Player D	1,000	4th $0	$133.21

These calculations are based on a standard full-ring sitngo, but they can be used to determine $EV in any format simply by substituting the relevant payout information and stack sizes.

Once you understand how ICM works, you will be better off using a spreadsheet or program to perform the calculations. For example the ICM spreadsheet at www.chillin411.com/icmcalc.php allows you to enter information for up to five payout positions and stack sizes for ten players.

Players of the more popular sitngo formats often use programs like SitNGo Wizard and Sit And Go End Game Tools for ICM calculations. For non-standard formats, you will need to customize software or use an ICM spreadsheet. This additional work can be profitable, since the correct strategies are not as readily accessible. Throughout this book, we will look at how ICM relates to sitngo structures, and use it to determine optimal strategies.

Short-stacked Play

Most important decisions in sitngos are made once the blinds have gotten very high. In cash games and tournaments your stack is usually deep enough that you can raise to around three big blinds and continuation-bet on the flop without committing yourself. This becomes difficult when your stack drops below 15 big blinds, as your entire stack can quickly go into play after the flop when it's hard to gauge your strength. Neither should you limp in most situations when your stack is so short.

By process of elimination, your best option is to raise your short stack all-in, forcing your opponent to play for all your (or his) chips or fold. This is particularly true in sitngos where, for ICM reasons, most players will not call an all-in raise without a very strong hand. They prefer to wait for opportunities to move all-in themselves and win the blinds uncontested.

The all-in zone can be divided into three categories, based on stack size.

10-15 Big Blinds

This stack size is a no man's land between the ideal stack for pushing all-in and the point at which you can comfortably afford to make a normal raise and continuation bet without committing yourself. You should generally play few hands and move all-in with them when you do.

Skilled players can determine when to come in with smaller raises. This is generally when you have 12-15 big blinds and believe your opponents will seldom defend their blinds or re-raise lightly.

When you move all-in, it should be with a high-quality hand (or excellent position). You will be risking a lot to win a little, and will have limited fold equity against a player that has raised before you.

5-10 Big Blinds

This is the ideal stack size for moving all-in. It is large enough to apply pressure to your opponents and deny mediocre hands the pot odds to call, but risks few chips, so you can move all-in with a wide range in many situations. Most late-stage sitngo play takes place with these stack sizes. You should make every effort to maintain a stack of at least five big blinds. This retains your fold equity and allow you to frequently pick up chips without a showdown, even if it means moving all-in light sometimes when under blind pressure.

0-5 Big Blinds

This usually results either from an unsuccessful attempt to maintain a stack of 5-10 big blinds, or a lost push all-in. You now have little or no fold equity when you push all-in, so you will need to find a good hand or a player in the big blind under considerable chip pressure. Going through the blinds will cost 30 percent or more of your remaining chips in just one orbit. You must look for the best opportunity to shove, based on your hand, your stack size, the player in the big blind, the other stacks at the table and how soon you'll be in the blinds.

When playing non-standard sitngos it is important to adapt your play to the exact situation, and to understand that with a given stack size, hand ranges will vary according to the format and the other stacks. The proper move may depend on quirks in the format or your opponents' playing styles.

Chapter Two

Fundamental Poker Concepts

For most sitngo formats understanding raise-sizing, ICM and short-stacked strategies are the key factors in becoming successful. However, in formats where more play is required whilst the blinds are still low – such as heads-up and six-max games and high-stakes games where the blinds are deeper or longer (for example a Step 6 satellite on Pokerstars starts with 150 big blinds and 10 minute levels) – a more general understanding of poker theory is necessary. This will also allow you to play more profitably in other formats whilst the blinds are low.

Therefore we will now look at some fundamental poker concepts that will inform your decision making in the time before the blinds get very high and ensure that you have an understanding of deeper-stacked poker theory that will allow you to outmanoeuvre your opponents whilst avoiding making costly mistakes yourself. Even in the standard sitngo formats this is now vital, since the advances in ICM programs and availability of information on sitngos in recent years has brought most players much closer together in terms of general and late game strategy.

Tournament Strategy

The important facts to remember when playing any tournament or sitngo format are that you will have a limited chip stack and be playing relatively shallow-stacked compared to a cash game, where stacks are deep and can be replenished at any time. For this reason, cash game players, and anyone else wishing to understand the differences in strategy that they will need to implement when playing tournaments or sitngos, will have to reconsider the number of hands they wish to play, and the way in which they play them based on these facts. The adjustments necessary are however fairly simple to understand and implement.

First, because your chip stack is finite and losing a significant percentage of it will increasingly limit your ability to speculate in hands and maximize value and leverage against other players (since you will have less big blinds and be able to win less chips from them) you should therefore be cautious about playing hands that may have only a very small positive expectation. Instead be prepared to wait for better situations if you have time, rather than gambling for a large percentage of your stack early. Of course in some formats and situations the amount of time you can wait may be limited, or you may feel the need to accumulate chips early in order to have a chance of a good result, and therefore be more willing to gamble in marginal spots, but you should still always try to consider these options consciously and make a decision based on them.

Second, try to minimize the variance in the hands that you do play so that you maximize your opportunities to accumulate chips (at least until you have a large stack). For example, whereas raising in early position with a small pair or suited connectors might be standard play in a six-max cash game with deep stacks, it may be best avoided in a six-max sitngo. Similarly, while re-raising light in a cash game in position with many suited or connected hands is now a standard strategy, in a sitngo it is less advisable as risking elimination in a marginal spot in the early game is not desirable due to ICM considerations. Furthermore, it may cause you to miss better opportunities to accumulate chips later.

There are also some fundamental differences between different tournament formats that are important to understand and result in different tournament strategies being favoured. An example is the difference between a standard sitngo and a multi-table tournament. In the latter you will usually face large fields and need to accumulate many chips to even make the money (since only 10-15% of the field get paid) then need to accumulate even more to have a shot at making the final table. For this reason, good MTT players (especially online ones where the structures are generally faster) are often much more willing to gamble in marginal spots to accumulate chips in the early stages so that they can use them to their advantage later.

You can often show a profit in sitngos without accumulating several times your starting stack (for example, in a double-or-nothing game you may barely need to win any hands if other players are knocked out quickly). Avoiding marginal spots even where ICM suggests them to be profitable will often be the correct strategy if you have a good chance of making the money without gambling. Your prospects of doing this depend on the format you are playing, so in a large field or winner-takes-all sitngo you might revert to the more aggressive strategy.

Protection Versus Value

Anyone who has observed or listened to both tournament and cash game players will know that there are significant theoretical differences in how they approach the game and the play of hands post-flop. This means that players successful in one area often struggle to adapt to the other. Cash game players are usually more sophisticated in post-flop skills such as hand-reading and planning because they have more experience in these areas and play with deeper stacks, but even they will need to make some adjustments in their post-flop game in order to succeed in tournaments.

The reasons for this are based on the general principles of tournament strategy that we have already discussed, i.e. that you cannot rebuy in tournaments when you lose some or all of your chips and that you generally play with shorter stacks than in cash games. Because of these facets it therefore becomes more correct to protect your hand by betting and raising in certain situations in order to take the pot down at once. In a cash game you might prefer pot control or try to gain additional value, but in tournament play you can less afford to be outdrawn and the ratio of chips in your stack to those in the pot is lower than in a cash game, making them more valuable – especially since you cannot rebuy and they will give you extra leverage and time.

In a cash game you can rebuy and the stack-to-pot ratio is higher, so it is usually better play to try to gain value from worse hands through calling or pot-controlling. This protects your stack by avoiding building big pots in situations where worse hands are likely to fold and better ones stay in. Here the utility value of the extra chips is usually irrelevant since you can rebuy if you lose and your goal is to make the most money in the long term rather than take pots down early, even if it results in some tough decisions or bad beats.

Of course these are subtle differences, and there are both situations in tournaments where you will be happy to slow play and risk being outdrawn to gain extra value, and situations in cash games where you may be betting a hand for both value and protection or simply to try and take the pot down. But this concept forms the basis of the difference in strategy between tournament and cash game play and trying to understand and apply it in marginal situations will help you to move successfully between the different disciplines and develop a more nuanced understanding of poker theory in general.

Continuation Betting Versus Pot Control

Continuation betting refers to making a bet which continues your prior aggression in a hand – typically when you have raised before the flop and been called – in an attempt to use this momentum to take the pot down. Usually you will have missed the flop or flopped a marginal hand and for this reason most players tend to continuation bet and try to win the pot at once rather than trying to showdown a marginal or weak hand. They also bet their stronger hands too in the hope of getting action.

This strategy tends to work best in sitngos and faster-paced tournaments where all players are fairly short-stacked and play straightforwardly. This contrasts with deeper-stacked cash games and tournament strategy where players are more apt to pot control by checking the flop a higher percentage of the time in order to get their hand to showdown more cheaply. This avoids building a large pot with a marginal hand and thus protects their stack.

However, pot control is less effective when short-stacked for a number of reasons. Firstly, with stacks that are very short for most of the tournament it is not very effective at limiting the proportion of your stack that you can lose, since even after checking the flop your opponent can still usually threaten most of your stack by betting the turn and river. Next, whilst players in cash games are often more likely to check down hands like ace-high or weak pairs, players in tournaments tend to fight more for chips and react to another player checking back by betting the next street in an attempt to win the pot or simply as a reflex action. This is fine if you have a hand with which you are comfortable calling down, but calling down with a marginal hand for a large percentage of your stack can risk ruining your tournament. This can be especially disastrous in sitngos where you do not need to accumulate many chips – unless you are sure it is a profitable line and that you are happy to induce bets from your opponent.

Finally, because of general tournament strategy and the flat payout structures of most sitngos, players are far less likely to play back at you than in a deep-stacked cash game or multi-table tournament. This makes continuation betting a more effective strategy even with marginal hands like bottom or middle pair, since you will rarely be bluffed or floated by a worse hand and you deny your opponent the chance to bluff you later.

Of course however you should not be continuation betting 100% of the time even against very weak opponents and there are some situations where pot control becomes more important even in sitngos. In heads-up sitngos, for example, players will often have or make marginal hands. For this reason, and also the lack of ICM considerations to constrain your opponents' play, you should be much more wary of being floated or check-raise bluffed and thus pot control more. You will also be playing with deeper stacks for the most part in this format and the lack of ICM considerations means you can call down more easily since your only concern is being unable to rebuy.

Similarly in full-ring and six-max sitngos pot control may be useful in certain situations. Against very tight regulars you may wish to check reasonably strong hands back for deception and pot control if you are unlikely to get three streets of value from them, or bet the flop and check the turn for pot control, then bet the river. Against more aggressive or maniacal opponents – who are likely to give you some tough decisions – or against aggressive six-max players, you may also revert to pot control in a conventional fashion whilst the stacks are still deep and you flop a marginal hand on a co-ordinated board.

Finally you may also elect to not continuation bet in some circumstances where you have missed the flop but it is very coordinated and the chances of it having hit your opponent are so great that it is not worth bluffing since you will get so few folds. This is typically the case when regular players flat call your raises in certain situations and are very likely to have speculative hands that connect with boards that contain a lot of middling and/or suited cards, or against weaker players who are very loose and rarely fold. Here you may instead elect to try a delayed continuation bet on the turn if they check back the flop, or simply decide to surrender the hand. However, if you often make this play you should also sometimes check-raise a big hand or draw here in order to balance your play.

Showdown Value

Having a hand with showdown value means that it is better than average and likely to win against your opponent's range, but that it is not strong enough to bet for value and that you should therefore try to 'get to showdown' as cheaply as possible. Additionally, for a hand to have showdown value you should also believe that you are likely to be able to get to showdown frequently and cheaply based on the vulnerability of your hand, its ability to pick up outs, your position and how your opponent plays. Clearly therefore, a hand that is often best, but is very vulnerable and cannot call a lot of bets from an aggressive opponent out of position only has limited showdown value.

Deciding whether your hand has showdown value is most important in deeper stacked and heads-up play and relates to the topics discussed in the previous sections. As we have seen, as stacks get shorter the value of pot control diminishes, and trying to showdown hands cheaply can therefore often become less profitable against some opponents than betting to take the pot down – since your opponent can still make bets totalling a large percentage of your stack and make showing down a weak hand expensive.

Throughout a sitngo you should try to guage which of your opponents understands these concepts and has the ability to apply them. The corollary of trying to get a marginal hand to showdown cheaply is that you will usually be betting hands for value or as a bluff (or semi-bluff) on the later streets. However, you will still encounter players that do not understand these concepts and will merge their betting ranges, sometimes betting hands for value that are unlikely to get called by worse ones or bluffing with hands where only better hands will call. Understanding this will allow you to make calls in some circumstances where it may seem logical not to against a player with a better understanding of poker theory.

Hand Ranges

Throughout this book, as in *Secrets of Sitngos*, we discuss hand ranges when assessing your opponent's possible holdings. This generally is in relation to pre-flop all-in ranges in no-limit hold'em sitngos. For example, we might put an opponent on a range of 10-10+ and A-Q+, indicating all pairs tens and higher and all ace-queen or ace-king hands. This is easy to enter in a program like *Sit And Go End Game Tools* or *SitNGo Wiz* which use hand ranges, pot odds and ICM calculations to evaluate your decisions.

In non-standard sitngos, and especially in formats like heads-up or six- max, where there will be more hands played while the blinds are low and therefore more complex decisions, it will be necessary to think about hand ranges in much more depth and in relation to board texture as well as betting patterns, which will often enable you to narrow your opponents' ranges down to only a small number of hands by the river.

For example, in heads-up play an opponent on the button should normally play a very high percentage of his hands (perhaps 80-100 percent, depending on the circumstances) because of his positional advantage. Based on the board cards that come and his chosen line, parts of his range can gradually be eliminated. Most players will continuation bet with most of their range on the flop, but some players will exercise pot control with mid-strength hands and give up on very coordinated boards, and a few might occasionally check back monsters or draws. On the turn, many players will give up with nothing if their flop continuation bet was called and they practice pot control with medium-strength hands. When they bet they are usually now either barreling a draw, betting a scare card or betting for value with a strong hand.

By the river you will have a lot of information, and since competent opponents should either be betting for value or bluffing at this point, you simply need to consider all the information along with the river card and bet sizing to assess their range and make a decision. For example, players that bet all three streets are usually very polarized between strong hands and bluffs, as they would have checked a medium-strength hand at some point. You must consider their style and history and decide if they might bluff often enough to warrant a call.

Understanding hand ranges and how to apply them is also essential to a correct understanding of poker theory, and even when the cards are turned over in a hand you should always be thinking in terms of hand ranges rather than in terms of the actual hands shown, in order to avoid becoming 'results oriented'[2]. For ex-

---

[2] Like Schrodinger's cat, which is either alive or dead inside a box depending on an earlier random event but whose state is unknown until the box is opened, the actual hand your opponent has (and whether it beats you or not this time) should be considered irrelevant.

ample, one misconception regarding hand reading that is often repeated by un-sophisticated players is that if you call the turn and a blank comes on the river you then have to call again since if your hand was good on the turn it is still good after the river is dealt.

Of course this statement is a truism in itself, however you are not playing against an individual hand but a range of hands, and your opponent's hand range for betting the turn and checking the river will be different from that for betting both turn and river. Therefore it might sometimes be correct to call the turn and fold the river when the board does not seem to change, since both your opponent's hand range and his perception of your hand range have still changed and you do not believe he is trying to bluff often enough against your new hand range for calling to be profitable.

Rather you should try to conceptualize your opponent's hand range, some of which beats you and some of which does not, and play accordingly with little regard for the individual result, unless it contradicts your initial hypothesis of the correct hand range to have put him on.

Chapter Three

Advanced Poker Concepts

As you progress as a player it is also worth starting to consider some more advanced concepts that will aid you in whatever form of poker you play, but especially when playing against the same group of opponents on a regular basis, against tougher players at higher stakes, heads-up or when the stacks are very deep. Here you will need to expand your knowledge of the previous topics discussed to include some psychology and more intricate poker theory in order to continue winning, and we will address some of these considerations now.

Image, Game Flow and Adjustments

Once you reach a certain level in sitngos you will find that many players will have mastered the fundamentals. As you move up in stakes, and particularly if you want to play in higher-stakes games with buy-ins of $200 or more (or if you work your way up to the top of the Step Ladder), where you will encounter some of the best players in the world, you must consider factors that separate good players from great players.

Most important among these factors are image and game flow, which may refer to anything from a player's general tendencies to how two players have been playing against each other. These factors are important in a general way in lower stakes games, where knowing that a player is a maniac or that someone may be on tilt might help you. At higher stakes, intelligent players will scrutinize your play and history with them, and will also observe how you are likely to perceive them—and how all this affects your hand ranges in specific situations.

You need to think about a variety of things in key situations, in addition to the simple mechanics of the game. You must consider your own image, that of your opponents and your history with them. You must also consider how your opponents' decisions might be affected by what has happened in the short, medium and long term.

This is because players change gears, go in and out of tilt and remember history with opponents over different time periods. And, whilst this is true at all levels, in games where the standard of play is generally high, these factors – and understanding the psychology behind each player's actions – is vital as they are most likely to determine the long term winners and losers. For example, even regulars who play against each other every day in standard sitngos will have a good idea of their opponent's all-in and calling ranges and will attempt to make small adjustments to exploit them that will in turn lead the other player to re-adjust when he perceives a change.

This process tends to continue ad infinitum unless the situation has a clear optimal strategy, such as heads-up with high blinds, and since such situations are rare even in sitngos, understanding when and how to adjust is key, particularly in heads-up play, where there are many marginal situations and no ICM constraints.

Levelling

Another fundamental concept that becomes important as you play against more sophisticated players – or against the same group of regulars and in formats like heads-up or six-max sitngos – is levelling. This refers to trying to out-manoeuvre your opponent by being on a different level, being able to predict how they will play in advance and then responding appropriately. To understand this concept, consider how various types of poker players behave, and on what levels they play.

At the very lowest level are players who simply play their own cards with no regard for other factors. They often make outrageously bad calls or folds based on how loosely or tightly they play. They may be beginners with little understanding of the game, or more experienced players who have not developed their hand-reading skills and who tend to think in absolute rather than relative terms about hand strength.

At the next level are players who also start to ask themselves, "What do I think my opponent has?". This might be called second level thinking and demonstrates an ability to start considering hand strengths in relative terms. For example, if a very tight player re-raises you it would be natural to throw away even very good hands in some situations. Similarly if you reach the river and have only a weak top pair against a tight player who is unlikely to be bluffing or value betting with worse hands, then folding to a big bet would be logical rather than just calling because you have top pair.

However, even with second level thinking you are still assuming your opponent plays in a fairly predictable way, and whilst this is true of some weaker and average players, against stronger players it won't be the case. You therefore need to take things one step further to third level thinking and also ask, "What do I think my opponent thinks I have?". This is where poker starts to become a mind-game and a war of trying to out-level other intelligent players since the "I think he thinks I think" game can be extended to infinity. The goal therefore is to correctly guess what level your opponent is on and stay one step ahead by anticipating and countering his actions.

This type of thinking certainly relates less to sitngo play than cash games because of the general constraints of tournament play and ICM, but it still exists between regulars who will change strategies or frequencies in response to their opponents. You will therefore need to consider how often players are bluffing or floating early on, or min-raise stealing or re-stealing late and how these frequencies change based on various factors. Of course in heads-up sitngos there are no ICM considerations so play here is more versatile and levelling in the purest sense in post-flop situations becomes much more important.

For example, low-level players often employ the desperation river bluff. They raise before the flop, continuation bet having missed, check the turn and bluff the river. This line makes little sense and first-level players will often pick off bluffs here. However if a more intelligent player knows that this is a terrible spot to bluff, he may well occasionally try a bluff there for the very reason than an intelligent opponent will reason that he is more likely to be value betting thinly and fold.

Similarly in the late game of a standard sitngo you may be able to falsely telegraph hand strength by making a 'suspicious' raise size with an extremely weak hand or unusually short stack size as a blind steal when you would not call an all-in, which will balance out the times you do it with a very strong hand and give you an additional way of stealing the blinds. Even in the most mechanical formats like standard sitngos, you should therefore still be looking for opportunities like these and this sort of thinking is an important part of what separates winning mid-stakes players from winning high-stakes players.

Thin Value Betting

As discussed in previous chapters, most players understand the difference between value-betting and bluffing, and have some rough understanding of when and why to do either. But the higher up in stakes you move the more players you will encounter whose hand-reading abilities are more refined and are able to accurately put opponents on hand ranges and predict what they might do with parts of them based on factors like history and gameflow.

Against these players you will need to refine your play significantly if you want to succeed and make your bets less predictable. One way of doing this is to start making thinner value bets against players with whom you have some history and who are likely to look you up lightly in certain situations. This will have a number of advantages. Firstly, it will help de-polarize your hand ranges from ones where you are typically only betting with a very strong hand or a very weak one (which tends to bias it towards weakness since it is hard to make a big hand in hold'em), making you harder to read, and forcing other players to call you down with weaker holdings. Secondly it will make it easier for you to bluff in future since other players will have to consider that as well as betting a very strong hand or bluffing you might also be betting a slightly stronger hand for 'thin value'.

Now you need to consider the possibility of your opponent betting a very strong hand for value and one slightly stronger than your own as well as a bluff and, in some instances, maybe even one slightly weaker than yours. This concept can apply in all sorts of spots where the value betting ranges of weaker players might be overly polarized or where you face weaker players who like to call you down and don't allow for the possibility that you are betting a hand for value that they may not put in your range. It also helps significantly in protecting your bluffs since in hold'em it is rare to make hands that you can bet for value on multiple streets or on a very scary river and, by doing so, you add significantly to your value betting range and give it a better weighting against your bluffing range, which might otherwise make up too large a part of your overall hand-range to be profitable.

In sitngos this sort of thinking applies mainly to playing heads-up or with deeper stacks, but it is certainly occasionally worth employing in other areas in order to be less predictable. This is especially the case against regular opponents who may remember your actions in future situations and give you more credit for making thin value bets, which in turn will allow you to bluff slightly more often.

Playing the Turn

Previously we discussed the basic mechanics and theory of post-flop play and how to apply it to tournaments and sitngos, including adjusting your pre-flop play and continuation betting frequencies on the flop. However in order to continue winning against regular and tough opponents, you will sometimes need to continue applying aggression on the turn after playing aggressively on the flop. This entails following through on bluffs and semi-bluffs against players who sometimes float you or call with weak hands hoping you will give up (or check-raising against players who like to try and take pots away on the turn), and perhaps even betting thinly for value in situations where you have an aggressive dynamic with another player. Doing all of these things in some frequency will give you a more balanced game and make you difficult to play against and we will now look at some of the different scenarios you might find yourself in and how you might choose to play based on the different variables.

The most common situation is that you have raised before the flop and a player has called you both before and after the flop. You must consider your position at the table and relative to the other player, the texture of the flop and turn cards, your opponent's tendencies and the exact tournament situation. If you have raised in early position, then you may have a strong hand when the board comes high or uncoordinated, in which case you should bet the flop and turn in favorable situations. If the board is low or draw-heavy, then you might give up after one bet (or not even bet the flop). You should be more inclined to bluff when you are in position or if scare cards come on the turn, as both factors are in your favor.

If you have raised in late position and been called on the flop, then your position relative to the caller is very important. Few players are likely to float you out of position on the flop with no hand when you act last. Your opponent is therefore likely to have some part of the flop if he calls, but bear in mind that many will call pre-flop and on the flop with hands like medium pairs when the board is low, or if there is only one overcard. You should sometimes double- and even triple-barrel against these players when bad cards come. If you raised before the flop in late position and you are out of position on the flop, then your play should vary according to your opponent, as players at all levels have widely varying post-flop strategies.

Betting the turn in a tournament or sitngo may involve committing a significant portion of your stack and so you generally want to be able to make bets that can set you up to move all-in on the river without committing you to calling all-in on the turn – whether you intend to follow through or not. Again, you should look for good situations if you intend to bluff, such as dry, paired or ace-high boards where it is unlikely you can have a draw. You should not bet if you are unlikely to get a fold, such as when the board is very coordinated or the turn card may have improved some marginal hands with gutshots or other outs.

Your opponents in higher stakes games are likely to use similar tactics against you and therefore you will need to adjust to them. In order to achieve this you can do things like fold marginal hands out of position on the flop if they cannot stand turn aggression or may face many bad cards; call down lighter in position against players who like to barrel or bet scare cards too often or be prepared to make large or all-in raises on the turn with draws in situations where your opponent is likely to bet-fold a good portion of his range.

Unless you are very sure your opponents are weak and will often fold you should barrel or semi-bluff the turn much less frequently in formats where your expectation is highly dependent on ICM, such as double-or-nothing or multi-prize satellite formats, or where you are playing relatively short-stacked, as you will risk losing a significant portion of your stack on one hand. Against regular opponents in standard sitngos or in very propitious situations, you should employ these tactics occasionally to balance your game.

Conversely, you should employ turn aggression much more often in formats with no ICM considerations and deeper stacks, like heads-up sitngos, winner-take-all satellites and Step 6 tournaments, where most of the money goes to the top finisher and you need to accumulate chips rather than worry about losing them.

Playing the River

Playing the river might seem like a fairly simple situation as at this point in a hand all the cards are out so there are no future considerations except the final betting. If you are the aggressor you should either be betting for value or as a bluff and if you face a bet you simply need to consider the pot-odds you are getting and weigh these against the possibility that your opponent is bluffing (or maybe betting a slightly worse hand for value).

However within these options – and because in no limit hold'em players can bet small, bet the pot or even over-bet – river play becomes much more complex. Between good players psychology also plays an important part. The possibilities of bluff-raising and check-raise bluffing between very strong players make it an even more interesting street to consider. We have already discussed thin value betting which applies mostly on the river, and will assume most players understand how to bet a strong hand for value, however bluffing (and calling bluffs) is a more complex subject.

Typically on the river you will face a fairly straightforward situation where you must either call a bet with a marginal hand or consider making a bet yourself as a bluff when your hand is a loser. If you are facing the bet it will typically be between half- and full-pot giving you odds of between 2-to-1 and 3-to-1, which are good but not compelling and require you to think back through the hand to decide whether the possibility that your opponent is bluffing or value betting a worse hand often enough to make calling profitable.

In deciding this, the tendencies of your opponent and the betting on previous streets are almost as important as the hand you have since by the river you may be looking at a situation where two pair is almost never good or where ace-high is likely to be winning. Consider whether your opponent is credibly representing a holding that beats you based on his actions throughout the hand. For example, a bad player will often make desperation bluffs on the river that make no sense having continuation bet and checked the turn, but a strong player would only do this against another strong player who would see it as a terrible spot to bluff and fold. Similarly, players who bet throughout a hand but do not value bet thinly in other situations are polarizing their ranges to bluffs and very strong hands and if they have a tendency to bluff – or if the draws have missed – you should be inclined to make marginal calls against them and not fear large bets.

When you have a losing hand on the river you should not bluff unless you have a good read on your opponent or can represent a hand credibly (again a trait of me-diocre players is not knowing when to give up). Think back through the hand – your action, the cards that came, and your dynamic with the opponent – and base your decision on that. Usually you will find yourself in good bluffing spots that develop during a hand based on the action from previous streets to the river (e.g. as scare cards and overcards arrive, but your draw misses), at which point you can evaluate the situation and your opponent's range and consider whether a bet is profitable. If you are going to bet between half- and full-pot you are giving your-self odds of between 2-to-1 and even money to win so you don't need to get your opponent to fold that often to win. Bluffing is also very important for metagame purposes, so if you were to break even on bluffing you would be still be happy.

These are the situations that usually unfold in hands and the ones you will face frequently. However you will also find yourself in more unusual situations from time to time, typically against very good or very bad players. Bad players (and even some 'good' tournament players) can be awkward to play against as they often make bets based on faulty reasoning, or of an unusual size. For example, they will bet a hand with showdown value but that will never get called by a worse one, or make a 'blocking' bet with a medium strength hand in the hopes of not having to face a larger bet.

Against such players you will simply have to take the information you have about them, try to understand their logic and then act accordingly. Perhaps a bad player makes small river bets giving you good odds so you will need to call with many hands as he sometimes makes foolish bluffs (whereas a good player would usually bluff bigger). Or alternatively when a mediocre player makes a blocking bet you can move all-in as they have telegraphed the strength of their hand and will fold if you give them the 'wrong' information and raise.

Very good players present a different set of problems as their bluffs will usually be balanced, consistent with the big hands they are representing and well timed. For this reason, playing guessing games against a strong player is a losing proposition and you should try to avoid the predicament by not playing many pots out of posi-tion with marginal hands against them in the first place. However when you do, psychology and history will become important factors and you should rely heavily on them as your opponent will often have a good read on your hand strength and will be focused on how you are likely to play. Now you might be more inclined to call lighter when overcards or scare cards come if their range is wide and they are likely to use them to bluff you, or call in spots where they know that you know their bet makes no sense.

Even more elaborate are lines that involve bluff-raising or check-raising the river. These should only be attempted against players capable of folding hands because they are competent hand readers or overly tight and you have a good read on them and their hand range. Again, making (or calling against) these plays relies on hand ranges and pot-odds, but check-raise bluffing the river is an excellent deep-stacked play against opponents that like to value bet thinly when some kind of draw has hit that you might have played that way and will force them to check more hands down in future. Similarly, you yourself should be careful of making thin bets against players capable of such bluffs, or at least be prepared to pick them off if a good spot comes up.

As with most of the topics in this chapter, river bluffing and making big calls with marginal hands is most applicable to games where ICM does not play a big part or where the stacks are deep. In shallow-stacked games losing a significant portion of your chips on a bad river play can be very costly as it limits your leverage over other players and your ability to come back and win the sitngo and this is even more the case if you did not need to accumulate chips in the first place. However, making good calls and bluffs will be an essential part of heads up play and you will also encounter situations in other formats where it is appropriate. Therefore thinking about it and practising it as much as possible is essential for high level play as long as you remember what is at stake in each individual situation and factor that into your decision.

Chapter Four

Non-standard Sitngo Formats

Many new and non-standard sitngo formats have appeared in recent years. Some take place regularly at higher stakes on most sites whereas others only usually fill at lower stakes or are restricted to certain sites. Experiment and find formats that suit your strengths and the stakes you want to play for. Some understanding of other formats will help you to understand ICM and poker theory and to think about adjustments required. These formats will give you something to fall back on if you want to change your game due to availability or profitability of your chosen sitngo formats.

Heads-up Sitngos

One of the most popular forms of sitngos on the Internet has always been heads-up, where only two players enter a game for a fixed amount, playing until one of them has all the chips and takes all the prize money. They balance the skill of heads-up cash-game play with the fixed buy-in of a tournament, ensuring that players will not lose too much or be able to leave after a few hands if they don't like their opponent. The rapidly changing stack sizes and increasing blinds allow for some strategy changes that are unique to this very specialized format. Many players have done well in heads-up sitngos, which are popular among recreational players. Currently they are available online for stakes as high as $5,600.

Heads-up sitngo strategy is radically different than that for standard sitngos or ring games. Because there is only one prize, ICM considerations do not apply and your chips have a fixed value. Hence, in a $15 game with 1,500 chips, each chip will always be worth one cent. And because there are only two players and you must post the blinds every hand, you will need to play a large number of hands to avoid being blinded away.

The Early Game

The number of hands you play depends primarily on your position, but also on your opponent and the size of the stacks. Players typically start heads-up sitngos with 1,500 chips and have stacks of 50 or 75 big blinds, which is reasonably deep. Initially, you should be raising most hands on the button in order to put pressure on your opponent and keep picking up the blinds, which means frequently playing marginal hands like Q-9o, K-2s, 7-5o and 10-3s. You can adjust this strategy, playing almost all hands if your opponent is too tight, perhaps making a few token folds so that he doesn't catch on, or tightening up if your opponent is very loose or aggressive. But you should generally play a very high percentage of your starting hands in position, typically 80-100 percent.

The standard raise for openers is three big blinds, but a raise of 1-2.5 blinds is viable. Min-raising encourages action and is preferable if you like playing post-flop, or if your opponent is particularly tight or aggressive, since stealing his big blind will cost fewer chips.

Raising to 2.5 big blinds is increasingly popular. It lessens your opponent's ability to defend correctly, since he gets odds of 7-to-3 instead of 3-to-1. It's much cheaper than the traditional raise and makes it harder for your opponent to decide whether to defend liberally.

Some players favor some degree of limping. With this strategy it is important to have a very balanced range, limping with big and small hands, and also limp-reraising with a balanced range. This is hard to achieve, and is therefore not recommended, but it work well against very aggressive or tilting players as a means of countering their style and frustrating them.

With stacks this deep, you don't want to call with many marginal hands out of position, as your opponent will be able to put a lot of pressure on you post-flop by betting multiple streets. But you can three-bet bluff against a player who opens very wide, and extract value from your big hands. For the most part though, because of the fixed stack sizes in heads-up sitngos, you should call more than re-raise, since losing even one large pot will put you in a tough spot. For example, if you lose a big pot early and end up with 1,000 chips to your opponent's 2,000, you now have to win two large pots to end the match, and you have fewer big blinds to work with and less leverage over your opponent.

By just calling with very big hands like A-A or K-K more often than in a cash game, you balance the other hands you wish to call with, such as suited aces and connectors, high cards and small or medium pairs. Hands like ace-rag offsuit and very weak connected or suited cards are difficult to defend when out of position, although increased pot odds and a smaller pot size make them playable against min-raises from the button.

It's good to sometimes re-raise, but you should lean toward hands that flop well like A-Q+, 9-9+ and high suited connectors. Pay attention to the flow of the game, and try to base your strategy on this, so if you have already re-raised a few times and then find aces, you should re-raise again, since your opponent will perceive you as more active than you are. But if you have not re-raised much, or it is early in the game, flat-calling may be better in order to not waste a big hand. You can adjust your strategy as the stacks start to diversify. For example, if you gain a lead of 1,800 vs. 1,200, then you can re-raise more liberally, since losing the 300 chips you have gained does not affect your leverage over your opponent.

Before calling a re-raise or four-betting all-in, you must carefully consider your opponent's hand range, which can vary significantly depending on stack sizes. Even with stacks of 50-75 big blinds, you can't afford to call re-raises with too many speculative hands unless your opponent is re-raising very wide. Implied odds are quite poor post-flop compared to a cash game, where stacks are typically 100 big blinds or more. If you do so, it should be with big suited connectors, big pairs that you wish to trap with and hands such as A-Jo or A-10s that are too big to fold but are not quite strong enough for a push.

When considering whether to re-raise all-in, or when to call a shove, much of the math can be done using PokerStove. Players should use this free program as much as possible in order to become familiar with the mechanics of the game, since these are mainly math problems.

For example, say the blinds are 10/20 and the effective stacks are 1,000. Player A re-raises Players B's open to 200, and Player B shoves. Player A is getting odds of 1,200-to-800 to call, and must therefore win 40 percent of the time to show a profit. If we assume that Player A has re-raised with 9-9, then we can use Poker-

Stove to find out what hand ranges would have this equity against his hand and determine whether we think Player B is shoving lighter than that. For example, Player A has about 41-percent equity against 9-9+, A-J+. This drops to 38.5 percent if Player B only moves all-in with 9-9+, A-Js+, A-Qo+. But adding 8-8 to that range increases Player A's equity to almost 42 percent, in which case he should call.

You should usually continuation-bet in position unless your opponent plays back at you or calls lightly a lot. Try to make logical decisions about when to go for value, control the pot or bluff, based on your hand strength and how your opponent plays. Pot control is a useful tool in deeper-stacked games and in heads-up play, but only against sophisticated opponents who will play back at you. If your opponent responds straightforwardly to continuation-bets, then your best option is to bet-fold many of your marginal hands, since you will usually be beat, or only control the pot with them on draw-heavy boards where you might face a flush or straight draw.

Planning the hand enables you to decide early on whether to continuation-bet and fold to action or try to get a hand to showdown cheaply, when to double-barrel on the turn, how to respond to a raise and how to play if certain cards come. Planning helps you avoid tough spots. The most important tools for heads-up play are knowledge of poker theory, hand reading and relative hand values, plus the ability to learn about and adapt to your opponents.

Out of position post-flop, you are very vulnerable because your opponent always acts last, and in deeper-stacked games will generally be able to fire three barrels at you. You should have already selected a stronger range of hands to play, which should keep you out of most tough situations. You will need to continue applying poker theory, hand reading and opponent profiling to your situation and think through your plan for the hand.

With most of your middle-strength hands, you should call continuation bets to gain value against worse hands and future bluffs, and polarize your check-raises to strong hands, draws, bluffs, and hands with some value that will be hard to showdown. Observe your opponent's opening- and continuation-betting frequencies in doing this, as well as his expected turn and river strategies. You will need to readjust this hand range as the hand progresses.

In a re-raised pot, you will need to again consider your opponent's hand range and stack size, although leading out with a bet of around half the pot is a standard line. Consider checking against aggressive opponents or on terrible flops, so as not to be too predictable. Also check with very strong hands and draws so that you can trap or check-raise.

If you have re-raised with a hand like 9-9, you may prefer to check-raise all-in on some awkward flops, such as those with one non-ace overcard, rather than bet-fold or bet-call, if your opponent is likely to stab at the flop when you check and you have the appropriate stack size.

The Middle Game

Stack sizes will naturally become shallower as play progresses, since either one player is winning or the blinds have gone up. With 15-30 big blinds, you are in an awkward position. Consider lowering your raise size to 2.5x. Limp sometimes to avoid big pots, or if your opponent often re-raises all-in. People often play more cautiously at this stage because losing even a couple of small pots can severely curtail your chances of winning.

When people limp, it's viable to stab at a lot of pots post-flop either in or out of position with a bet of half- to 3/4-pot, as your opponent will rarely have hit. Balance this with value bets and check-raises, adjusting based on your opponent's response. Winning just a few of these pots can give you a chip lead, allowing you to gamble without falling behind. If your opponent opens a lot pre-flop, then re-raising all-in with pairs, high cards and some suited connectors is a great way to cut him down, as he will rarely be able to call.

The Late Game

As the average stack falls below 15 big blinds, you will again need to adjust your strategy. Against a very weak player and with deeper stacks you should generally apply a small-ball strategy that consists of limping or making small raises and playing post-flop, but with shorter stacks and against tougher opponents you should shove or fold, and against very tough players employ a game theory optimal strategy that has no defense.

Your approach and the frequency with which you take certain actions should depend on your opponent. With stacks of 15 (or perhaps 12.5) big blinds or more, raising to 2.5 big blinds pre-flop rather than moving all-in is obviously superior if your opponent will fold similar ranges of hands to both actions. But it is less ideal if he will re-raise with a wider range in the belief that you will fold often, in which case you might simply open with a tighter range and call his re-raises with a wider one, or revert to a jam-or-fold strategy to deny him any fold equity. By contrast, limping on the button to control the pot size is ideal against loose-passive opponents who you figure you can outplay later.

With stacks below 15 big blinds, and especially below 10 big blinds, when it becomes optimal to either jam or fold, you should play small-ball only against highly exploitable players. These consist primarily of loose-passive players with poor post-flop skills, and tight players who will fold a wide range of hands to a small raise.

When you have less than 15 big blinds and face a tough or unknown opponent (or if you are inexperienced) you should usually adopt a jam-or fold strategy that forces your foe to commit all his chips or forfeit the blinds. This might be based on your opponent's tendencies if he is very exploitable (e.g., someone who folds too much) or on a game theory optimal strategy that will combat tougher heads-up opponents who have a good understanding of such strategy.

Bill Chen and Jerrod Ankenman have formulated jam-or-fold tables for game theory optimal play when heads-up with high blinds. These are found in their groundbreaking work, *The Mathematics of Poker*, and are reprinted in *Secrets of Sitngos*.

These tables show how far from optimal are most players' heads-up strategies, and reveal much about the comparative values of hands in different situations. For example, with stacks of 15 big blinds or less, any ace or pair is not only an automatic all-in (which most players understand), but also an automatic call because the wide shoving range of an optimally playing opponent means these hands will rarely be dominated even when as marginal as A-2 or 2-2.

Similarly, while most players understand the value of suited connectors as all-in hands, these tables show the extent to which unsuited connectors and suited non-connected cards are undervalued. For example, 8-7 offsuit and J-5 suited are both profitable when moving all-in with 15 big-blind stacks against an optimally playing opponent, simply because (as with suited connectors) you will win the blinds often enough to compensate for the times you are called by a superior hand, and even then, you will still have reasonable equity against calling ranges weighted towards high cards and pairs.

A complete explanation of the method used to determine these tables can be found in *The Mathematics of Poker*, along with jam-or-fold tables for stacks of up to 50 big blinds. In practice, you should almost never use a jam-or-fold strategy with a stack greater than 20 big blinds, and instead be prepared to play small ball. We previously defined the all-in zone as 15 big blinds or less, but when heads-up against tough or aggressive opponents (or if you are very inexperienced), jamming with hands like 2-2 or A-2 that will be tough to play post-flop, or hands like Q-Jo that can't call a re-raise is acceptable with stacks as big as 20 big blinds.

You should note however that whilst these tables lay out a game theory optimal strategy which will negate any advantage a strong or unknown opponent might have against you, it will be correct to diverge from them against opponents who are much too tight or too loose in order to play an optimal exploitative strategy, (i.e. one which is tailored to your opponents weaknesses). For example, against an opponent who only plays very big hands and has not adjusted well to head-up play you can move all-in with a much wider range than in these tables as you will almost always win the blinds, but you should call an all-in with far fewer hands than they recommend as he will not be moving all-in optimally.

Six-max Sitngos

Six-max sitngos have become increasingly popular, since they require fewer players to start and allow for more action in the early stages. If you are going to play this format, you should be more confident in your ability to "play poker" and make post-flop decisions, because the blinds will pass through you more frequently and you will not be able to sit back during the early game as much as you would in a full-table sitngo. This will be even truer as players are eliminated and the game becomes very short-handed. You will often reach the bubble with relatively deep stacks compared to a full-ring sitngo, so you will need to play post-flop at that stage as well.

Six-max sitngos usually only pay the top two players, typically with a 65/35 split between first and second place. This requires some strategy adjustments according to ICM.

When all are in the money in a standard full-ring sitngo, the three winners will share the prize pool on a 50/30/20 basis, i.e., three players are guaranteed 20 percent each, with the final 40 percent of the prize pool divided between them on a 75/25/0 basis (30 percent of the total pool to first place, 10 percent to second and zero to third).

With a standard six-max sitngo paying 65/35/0, you have a much greater incentive to play for the money (unless you have a dominating lead) than you would to creep up into second when three-handed in a full-ring sitngo. If we consider a six-max $100 sitngo with payouts of $390 for first and $210 for second, then with equal stacks on the bubble each player will have a $EV of $200, but if one doubles through another this alters to:

Player	Stack Size	Tournament Equity ($EV)
Player A	6,000	$330
Player B	3,000	$270
Player C	0	$0

There is significant equity leakage when the bubble bursts in this format, since 70 percent (or $420) of the prize pool is now allocated and the remaining players are only competing for $180. It is not as serious as on the bubble of a standard sitngo where four players remain and only three get paid, but to play an all-in at this stage you must still be a significant favorite (excluding the presence of blinds and antes), as your equity when all have equal stacks is $200/$330 = 60.61 percent.

Things get more interesting in this format when one big stack dominates two shorter stacks, since there is now a huge incentive for the short stacks to get past the bubble. Consider the following scenario:

Player	Stack Size	Tournament Equity ($EV)
Player A	6,000	$316
Player B	1,500	$142
Player C	1,500	$142

Here the big stack is utterly dominant and should be moving all-in almost every hand to exploit the bubble effect (unless the big blind commits a player to calling with a wide range and he has a very weak hand), since a shorter stack's equity increases little even if he wins.

Player	Stack Size	Tournament Equity ($EV)
Player A	4,500	$268.50
Player B	3,000	$214
Player C	1,500	$117.50

With equity of $142/$214 = 66.36 percent, the short stack will rarely be a sufficient favorite against the big stack's range to warrant a call.

Each short stack has a strong incentive to wait for the other to be eliminated because his equity will increase from $142 to $240, as we see in the following table.

Player	Stack Size	Tournament Equity ($EV)
Player A	7,500	$360
Player B	1,500	$240
Player C	0	$0

This demonstrates that in six-max sitngos when one player achieves a dominating stack on the bubble, he is in an excellent position to exploit the other two players, who should want to avoid confrontation with him and wait for the other's elimination. Because of this, and because a dominating stack is easier to achieve in a six-max game than in a full-ring sitngo, it is often worthwhile to attempt to build a big stack early, particularly since close gambles at that stage will have a slightly less negative $EV than in a full-ring game with three prizes. For example, a player who doubles up early in a six-max sitngo will have slightly more equity that the $184.48 he would in a full-ring contest.

(see following table)

You should not look to achieve this by taking the first all-in opportunity, since a coin flip would still have negative expectation, but you should employ a more aggressive strategy and be more willing to play all-in with hands like strong draws. You will either force opponents to fold marginal hands, thereby increasing your stack, or you will be all-in, resulting either in your getting a big stack or being eliminated. If you win, then you will be in a good position to work towards bubble domination; if you lose, your equity loss is minimal and you will be more than compensated when you make other players fold or get them to put their chips in badly when you have a strong made hand.

Player	Stack Size	Tournament Equity ($EV)
Player A	1,500	$103.5
Player B	1,500	$103.5
Player C	1,500	$103.5
Player D	1,500	$103.5
Player E	3,000	$186

The Early Game

You must play more hands in the early stages of a six-max sitngo than in a full ring. With players getting involved in more pots and being eliminated quicker in this format, you are likely to lose a significant portion of your chips if you don't get involved early.

Because a chip lead on the bubble in a six-max sitngo is very powerful, you should be willing to get involved a little more to maximize your chances of building a big stack. If you start with 1,500 chips, losing a few and going down to around 1,000-1,200 isn't a massive problem, as you can start playing push-or-fold at the 50/100 level. But you can exercise significant leverage if you make it up to 2,000-3,000 chips.

You should play relatively loosely in the early stages, opening hands like mid-high pairs, good or suited aces and good suited connectors from most positions. Try to get in pots with bad players, as they will likely lose their money quickly. In late po-sition, you can raise with hands like low or gapped suited connectors, weak aces and face cards, hoping to use your position to win pots. You should still play tighter than in a cash game because you cannot re-buy. Hence, opening with hands like small pairs or low suited-connectors in the first two positions is best avoided, as they play poorly post-flop.

Be wary of re-raising with medium-strength hands, especially out of position; with stacks of 50-75 big blinds you will often find yourself in awkward spots post-flop with hands like 8-8 or A-10. Instead, play smaller pots in position with these hands as much as possible while the blinds are low, or at least until you build up a lead. When you do flop a hand like a good draw in the six-max format, you should play it more aggressively than in a full-ring sitngo. A chip lead is very beneficial, and ICM dictates that going all-in is not the problem in the six-max format that is in full-ring. Players will have wider hand ranges, giving you more fold equity in this format, and with only six stacks in play, it's easier to build a dominating stack than in a full-ring sitngo.

The Middle Game

While the blinds increase, players will be eliminated and stack sizes will start to diversify. You will need to adapt your strategy to the new situation and the size of the blinds relative to your stack. You should play fewer speculative hands as your pot odds decrease, and think more about stack sizes when re-raising. If you lost chips early on, your best strategy is often to play very tightly until you reach a level where you can play jam-or-fold. With a larger stack, you can play more aggressively and steal from shorter-stacked players.

As players are knocked out and the game develops, you will start to form an idea of what the endgame around the bubble will look like, and what you will need to do to cash or win. If one big stack develops quickly, you can often sit on a reasonably-sized stack and hope to sneak into the money, but if a couple of players double up, then you will likely want to do the same as you head toward the bubble. Play a few more hands in the middle game with this in mind, or be prepared to re-raise all-in a bit lighter.

The Bubble

When you get down to three players in a six-max sitngo, the game flow will be even more dictated by the stack sizes than in a full-ring sitngo with four players on the bubble. With only two opponents, a big stack can dominate much more easily because he's less likely to encounter a hand or face a raise, and because playing to make the money is preferable to risking everything for the win if there are two short stacks and one big one.

If you are the big stack, you should make frequent small raises if your opponents have stacks greater than 15 big blinds, and shove most of the time when first to act if they have less than ten big blinds and you have over three times their stack size, assuming your opponents are competent and understand bubble strategy. Otherwise, you should push a few less hands and watch for players who become frustrated, a common occurrence in six-max because the bubble can be quite intense and personal with only three players. Some players try to become the big stack by calling looser than ICM suggests. Watch out for these players if they can double through you into the lead. Shove more tightly or make small raises instead.

Play aggressively whenever you have a slight lead, the goal being to surge into a dominating position. Do the same if the big stack is passive and you are able to overtake him with well-timed moves, or if the stacks are even and the play is tight or passive. The further you get in front, the more aggressive you can be. When your stack dominates the others and you are unlikely to be eliminated, then you can really bully the table. For example, with a stack of 6,000 against two stacks of 1,500, you are in an utterly dominant position. You can attack relentlessly even if an opponent doubles up.

With the second-place stack, you should play very few hands when there is an aggressive big stack, as it would be a disaster to be knocked out at this point. Use your chip lead over the third-place player as a buffer; wait him out and force him to risk an all-in before you do, unless you're dealt a very strong hand or can take him on yourself. For example, if you have 3,000 chips and your opponents have 4,500 and 1,500, losing 500 chips in the blinds is only 1/6 of your stack, but it's 1/3 of the shortest stack. If you both lose 500, then your stack is still 2.5 times his.

With the shortest stack, you must play aggressively and keep yourself in contention by not dropping to a point where you have less than half the second-place stack. You will typically play jam-or-fold. Use this leverage to attack the big blind of the second-place player. Try to get all-in with him instead of the big stack unless you have a strong hand. Winning this confrontation will reverse the chip positions and make you a comfortable second. Don't let yourself drop below five big blinds—be prepared to move all-in very wide in this quest, especially against the second-place player.

Above all, remember that your stack size dictates your bubble strategy in a six-max sitngo, and that when you are not the chip leader you should focus on the second- or third-place stack, trying to outlast him by forcing him to move all-in first if you are in front, trying to keep pace with him if you are even and attacking him if you are behind. This is by far the most important adjustment to six-max play. If you do it successfully, you will usually profit from weaker opponents or players who are strong in other areas but who do not make the correct adjustments.

Two-table Sitngos

Two-table sitngos typically consist of 18-20 players, and pay four places on a 40/30/20/10 structure. You should play normal tournament poker in the early and middle stages. You want to at least double or triple your stack during this time to have a chance at cashing; you can bet thinner values because you risk less equity in the early game. However, once you get close to the money, the relative flatness of the payout structure provides less incentive to play for first than in other formats. Even if you creep into second and lose to a massive stack, you will still receive 75 percent of the prize money he gets.

The payout structure provides much less incentive to build a dominating stack in a two-table sitngo than in a six-max contest (it would also be considerably harder). You should avoid close gambles in the late stages, since the equity loss will be massive. For example, say five players are left in a 20-player $100 sitngo, each with $400 in equity. If one doubles through another he only increases his equity by 50%:

Player	Stack Size	Tournament Equity ($EV)
Player A	12,000	$600
Player B	6,000	$466.67
Player C	6,000	$466.67
Player D	6,000	$466.66

Player 1 would have to be a 66.66-percent favorite (excluding blinds and antes) to have positive expectation.

$400/$600 = 66.66\%$

It's generally correct at this stage to play a cautious and patient game in the hope that the elimination of other players will allow you to move up. Exceptions occur when you are in last place, risk being blinded away or have the dominant stack (in which case you wield enormous leverage).

The Early Game

It is important to open up your game a little early on. Fewer than 1/4 of the players will cash in a two-table sitngo, and in the beginning you will tend to see several weak players. You want their chips, and you can stack these players with less risk when the blinds are low. You need to accumulate chips—players who cash average 4.5-5 times the starting stack size—and now is the time to start.

Your first job is to identify the weaker players. You can eliminate the solid regulars, and then determine who plays too many hands, makes strange bet sizes, etc. Try to play your marginal hands against these players; they will play worse than you and will start with hands even more marginal than yours. Suited connectors and small pairs are good candidates, and Broadway hands like K-10o and Q-Jo go up in value because weaker players often play hands like K-6o or Q-8o. You should still aim for quality hands, and you should play marginal hands cheaply and in position, preferably when other players have limped first.

The Middle Game

As players are eliminated, you will play shorthanded until the two tables consolidate into a final table of nine or ten players (so you will be playing five- or six-handed immediately beforehand). If you have a short or medium stack that can survive until the final table, you should make fewer marginal all-in moves because once you get to the final table, you will only have to pay the big blind once every nine or ten hands, allowing you to wait for better opportunities. But if you have a big stack and sense that the other players are being too cautious, you should use your leverage to accumulate more chips while there are fewer opponents to steal through.

At the final table, you will need to think about your prospects for making the money and how your stack size relates to the blind structure, so that you can maintain enough fold equity to keep stealing the blinds (for example, on Poker-Stars there is a big leap between the 100/200/a25 and 200/400/a25 levels). Keeping above five big blinds at these levels is even more important at this stage, as you still have a way to go to the money, so assess the stack sizes at the table and look for good opportunities to steal against mid-sized stacks. Note any stacks above 6,750, which will reduce the average for the other three players who get paid and make things a bit easier for you if you are short-stacked.

The Late Stages

As the bubble approaches, pay close attention to your overall position and bear in mind the payout structure and ICM implications. With four players getting paid on a 40/30/20/10 basis, you win an extra ten percent of the prize pool for each position you advance beyond fifth. You should play differently than with a 50/30/20 structure, where there is a big leap from fourth to third and another from second to first.

In the late stages, your emphasis should usually be on survival. Avoid marginal all-ins. Try to pick up chips where there is minimal risk or when you are against shorter stacks. Calling with weak ace-high hands or small pairs is therefore not usually advisable. If you are in second place and the big stack pushes all-in, you may fold some mid-high pairs and strong aces. However, if other players are adopting this strategy, you can keep your stack healthy by moving all-in against them.

Play aggressively only with a very large stack that can lose an all-in with minimal damage. This is an excellent situation for you, as the others will tend to compete among themselves for the lower places and you will have a good chance to win. Don't be overly concerned about putting yourself in this position, since you will effectively be doing the work for the players who finish close behind you and re-ceive three-quarters or half your prize money for second or third.

By contrast, with a short stack that is in danger of missing the money, you have more incentive to gamble than in the standard format. Placing second or third pays two or three times as much as limping into fourth. You should attack the players already in the lower money positions who will not want risk their positions without a good hand. If you're successful and make second or third place, you can revert to playing to your stack size and avoid risky confrontations.

When back in the money, bear in mind these considerations when making mar-ginal shoves or calls, unless you have a very big stack. For example, three-handed in a normal sitngo, an additional 10 percent goes to second place, but 30 percent more to first, motivating you to play for the win, but in the two-table format, you get as much for advancing from third to second as from second to first. In this format then, and almost uniquely among tournaments, moving up the ladder is more important than playing to win. Survival is paramount here, hence this format will suit more solid and steady players.

Multi-table Sitngos

The success of the two-table format has motivated most poker sites to offer sitngos resembling multi-table tournaments, except that they start as soon as the required number of players register, and usually operate on a turbo structure so that they finish in a reasonable time. Because there are only a limited number of good regulars online at any time, these games can offer far higher ROIs than normal sitngos, although the variance is also greater.

Multi-table sitngos are usually offered in 45-, 90- and 180-player formats. Their popularity and frequency depend on the stakes and number of players. For example, 45-player sitngos at the $60 level are reasonably frequent, but 90- and 180-man games rarely run at high buy-ins. They are therefore a good place to cut your teeth if you are learning the game or want to practice for MTTs, and they allow you to build a bankroll fairly quickly if you have a few early results.

Payouts vary between sites and field sizes; check these details and estimate the average stack you will need to make the money. For example, seven places are paid in a 45-player game on PokerStars, so you will need to build your starting stack of 1,500 to around 10,000 to be about average, whereas you'll need more like 15,000 at the 180-player game on Full Tilt, which pays 18.

You will need to accumulate a lot of chips in a short time, so it's worth getting into early pots with speculative hands to get chips from the weaker players before they bust. ICM is much less relevant than in the single-table format, as the payouts are further away and increase more smoothly. Hence, you can play draws more aggressively and develop a looser image.

Most players will come under great chip pressure fairly quickly due to the fast structure of these games. Even with a big stack, you will be playing shove-or-fold with lots of players having fewer than ten big blinds. For this reason, stealing to keep above the all-in zone isn't as important in the middle game as in traditional MTTs. You should still look for good spots, particularly when the antes kick in and the stack sizes are such that opponents can't re-steal against you light very much but you can still fold marginal hands if they move all-in.

Look to move all-in aggressively even in marginal situations when the stacks get very short, as most players in these formats fold too much (especially at the lower stakes). If you build a good stack this way, you can dominate your table as the bubble approaches. With a shorter stack, watch for blind increases, which can be significant. If you are comfortable, then wait for some shorter stacks to consolidate and don't force the action.

ICM and traditional tournament strategies become more important as you approach the money' play based on your stack size and position in the field. You should know the average stack to get past the bubble, but you still need to watch the standings. Some very big stacks will reduce the average for the rest, and you might comfortably make the money with a shallower stack.

You will need to win chips to make the cut with a shorter stack. Stay aggressive, and try to keep above five big blinds so that you have good fold equity. Pick on players who might fold too often in the big blind if they are tight or trying to survive with a medium stack.

The main payouts in these formats are in the top positions. For example, the top three finishers in a PokerStars 90-player game share 60 percent of the prize pool, whereas 6th-12th places each get no more than five percent. If you have a big stack near the bubble, you must play aggressively and steal from players trying to squeeze into the money. This is very different from the strategy required for the 18-player games with a more flat payout structure. If you can get some distance out front at this point, you can often ride the wave to the top three by picking up all the dead money, and will have to lose a series of all-ins to be knocked out.

When the bubble bursts, there is usually a period of rapid consolidation; be patient unless you pick up a hand or have a short stack, in which case you should be ready to gamble. The action usually slows down as the final table becomes shorthanded. You can steal and shove more liberally at this point, depending on the stack sizes. Unless players are immediately likely to bust and you have a medium stack, you should focus on the top positions and play aggressively to get there. ICM still carries some weight, so you should avoid very thin gambles.

When it's down to three contestants, play becomes similar to a traditional sitngo, and you should usually play to win. If you are unfamiliar with the format, you should know how many total chips are in play and your stack size in terms of big blinds. If you have experience at standard sitngos, this will help you to make the right decisions.

Winner-take-all Sitngos

Sometimes a sitngo has just one prize. This is often a single-table satellite to a tournament. It might also be part of a shootout tournament, each level of which consists of a number of single-table contests, with the winner of each going forward. For example, in a 1,000-player shootout there are three rounds. The first round consists of 100 10-player sitngos. Each winner moves forward to a second round of 10 tables, and those winners sit at the final table. You typically receive nothing if you are knocked out in the early rounds, but in later rounds there will be some prizes, making them more like traditional sitngos or multi-table tournaments.

Your strategy is fairly straightforward in winner-take-all sitngos. ICM is irrelevant, since your cEV and $EV[3] will always be equal. For example, if you start with 1,000 chips in a 10-player, $1,000, single-table satellite for a $10,000 event, then each chip will be worth $1 at every stage of the event. Bear in mind that you cannot re-buy, hence you should not gamble recklessly in close situations early on if you are a large favorite in the game. Be prepared to take slightly +cEV opportunities as they arise, since these will always be +$EV as well, and you must accumulate chips to win.

Multi-prize Sitngos

Multi-prize sitngos have been around for some time. Variations have appeared, such as double-or-nothing and step sitngos. We will look at ICM considerations and strategy adjustments for the general format before moving on to the variations. In this format, you must tailor your strategy to the payout structure, includ-

---

[3] A more detailed explanation of these terms can be found in *Secrets of Sitngos*

ing such considerations as whether there is more than one level of prize, how many prizes there are, and whether there are cash prizes for players who fail to win tournament seats in sitngos that offer those as prizes.

Use ICM to guide your play in more extreme situations. For example, if a ten-player, $1,100 satellite pays $1,000 to second place and a $10,000 tournament seat to first, then you will mostly want to play to win, since your cEV and your $EV are similar, although you might want to avoid very close +cEV gambles, which will sometimes be -$EV.

In an event that pays all winners equally, whether as tournament seats or cash prizes, your strategy as the bubble approaches should be more extreme, according to ICM, than any other we have considered. For example, in a 10-player $80 satellite where four players win entry to a $200 event and everyone else gets nothing, with five equally-stacked players remaining the situation would look like this:

Player	Stack Size	Tournament Equity ($EV)
Player A	3,000	$160
Player B	3,000	$160
Player C	3,000	$160
Player D	3,000	$160
Player E	3,000	$160

If two players go all-in here, then the equity leakage will be massive, since they will virtually guarantee the other players a prize. In this example, an all-in player will either gain $40 of equity by winning a $200 prize or lose $160 through elimination, meaning that he will need to be an 80-percent favorite to break even in equity terms, ignoring blinds and antes. Unless the blinds are high, the only hand he will be happy to call all-in with will be aces. Even kings only have equity of around 82.4 percent against a random hand.

Playing on the bubble in a sitngo offering multiple equal prizes requires you to juggle between waiting for others to be eliminated and maintaining a healthy chip stack while avoiding all-in confrontations. To succeed, you must observe the stack sizes around you, see who is in the most danger and try to let that player risk elimination first. You must know whose blinds you can steal, who you can safely move in against and who is likely to call too loosely, putting both of you at risk.

Double-or-nothing Sitngos

A popular new format, the double-or-nothing sitngo sees ten players enter, with five winning double their entry fee and the rest going empty-handed. They currently run regularly up to the $100 level, and since the prize is much less than can be won in other sitngo formats, the entry fee has been reduced substantially, so at the highest level on PokerStars you pay $100 + $4 for the turbo game.[4]

This format requires major strategy adjustments, since you get the same reward for making the final five with one chip or nearly all of them. Also, because half the field gets paid, the average chip stack when the bubble bursts will only be 3,000 (if the starting stacks are 1,500), so you may need to do very little to win. If one player builds a much larger stack, that's good news for you, as it reduces the amount required by the other players to win. For example, with one stack of 9,000 chips the average for the remaining winners would be 1,500, the same as they started with!

Avoid all-in situations at any point in a double-or-nothing sitngo unless you have a very strong hand or you are short-stacked and need to gamble to survive (this is increasingly true at lower stakes where other players may play badly and knock themselves out). ICM tells us that if you double up on the first hand of a $50 double-or-nothing sitngo, then your new stack of 3,000 chips is only worth $77.78, meaning that you would need to be all-in as more than a 64.3-percent favorite to show a profit.

This percentage increases dramatically as the bubble draws closer. If you get to the bubble with equal stacks, then each player will have $83.33 of equity. If an all-in confrontation occurs, then one player will win $100 and the other nothing, meaning that to go all-in you would need to be about an 83.33-percent (five-to-one) favorite.

---

[4] There is also a standard-speed format with a buy-in of $100 + 8, but at twice the rake of the turbo, it is not generally recommended.

This analysis makes it clear that a cautious approach is necessary for success at the double-or-nothing format. In the early stages, you should play small-ball with all but your strongest hands (even A-Ko is only a 65-percent favorite against a random hand) and look to amass chips before the blinds get high and you need to gamble. Look to do this through flopping big hands with holdings like pairs or suited connectors (when you can play them cheaply in position). Otherwise, there is little reason to get involved with marginal hands when you could win with little addition to your stack.

In the middle game you should assess your opponents' chip positions and develop an idea of what stack size you might need to win. With one or more large stacks, you will still be able to hang back and play only premium hands if you have your starting stack or a bit more, since the other small stacks will have few chips spread between them. But if some players have stacks of 2,000-3,000 and the rest of you have small stacks, then you will need to play a little more aggressively to keep pace. In this case, look for the tightest players to steal from or re-raise, and ramp this strategy up as antes come into play at the 25/50 level, when pots will be bigger and each orbit will cost you more.

As you approach the bubble, you will generally have a shallow stack, most players will play so as not to lose rather than to win, and you will mostly play a jam-or-fold game. Pay close attention to your chip position. Unless you are in last place, play very few hands—this forces players below you to make the first move and risk elimination. It's even correct to fold K-K to a shove with even stacks on the bubble of a double-or-nothing sitngo unless the blinds are very high and you face elimination first. If you are in close competition with other players, you should pay attention to the order of the blinds and imminent increases that may change your game plan.

If you encounter a marginal situation or an opportunity to steal in the late game, you should carefully consider the reward versus the risk based on the situation and the player you face. Be especially cautious if your opponents don't understand correct strategy and are likely to call with too many hands, hurting both of you. Extra chips are only useful in so far as they allow you to outlast other players. If you have a good chance of doing this anyway, it is pointless to put your tournament life at risk except with a very strong hand unless the other players also understand this.

Similarly, when someone else has moved all-in ahead of you, consider whether you need to get involved or have the correct odds to call even with an apparently strong hand. If you have a comfortable stack around the bubble, you can often let the other players fight it out, avoiding coin-flips even with fairly strong hands if losing might pull you back into the fray. Even with the right odds in this situation, if it is close, remember that other players will likely make mistakes that still make folding the best play. This sort of strategy (and the double-or-nothing format as a whole) might not be action-packed or full of fun, but it can be very profitable for players with patience and discipline.

Step Sitngos

Step tournaments run on a number of sites such as PokerStars and Party Poker. They have created a new way for players to qualify for major events like the European Poker Tour and the World Series of Poker Main Event. Players can buy in at various levels, trying to work their way up through each step, where the next level is about three times the buy-in of the previous one.

On PokerStars for example, there are six steps with buy-ins of $7.50, $27, $82, $215, $700 and $2,100. You can win a ticket to the next step, a ticket to the same step (or the one below) or nothing. The top step pays in entry packages or cash. For example, the Monte Carlo 2009 EPT Step 6 paid one package to first place and $1,200 to second place from the $20,000 prize pool, whereas the Punta del Este LAPT Step 6, with a smaller buy-in, pays in packages to the first three places and $500 to fourth place.[5]

Steps 1-5 have almost identical structures, offering two tickets to the step above and a variety of tickets to the same level or lower. The buy-in at the next level is about three times as much, hence about two-thirds of the prize pool is allocated there, with the rest going to the other prizes. This differs dramatically from a standard sitngo, where the payouts are split in a 50/30/20 proportion, and with a structure where only the winners show a profit, it's important to play for those places and not worry too much about the smaller prizes except in unusual situations.

---

[5] Due to new multi-currency options, some step tournaments are now played in Euros or Sterling, depending on the destination event.

You will need to accumulate chips at some early point in a step sitngo because in the endgame the big stacks will usually wait for the small one to be knocked out. With 13,500 chips in play in a nine-player game and starting stacks of 1,500 there will be an average of 4,500 for the last three players, and the winners will average 6,750. Play some speculative hands like small pairs and suited connectors, particularly against weak players who have come up from lower steps. ICM calculations confirm that gambling in the early stages of a step tournament is less problematic than in other sitngos. For example, doubling up your starting stack early in a Step 2 will take its value from $25 to $43.25, so while you still want to be a favorite to play all-in, you only need to be about 58 percent.

The more crucial strategy adjustments come when you enter the end game. With just two prizes, it is important on the bubble to not make a bad call and free-roll someone else into a prize. With three players left and two seats, if everyone has equal stacks, then each has two-thirds of a seat, and should an all-in occur, the players will each win an additional one-third or lose two-thirds (with the other third going to the third player).

You must be a 66.66% favorite to call in such a spot unless pot odds or high blinds play a large role, and when there are two large stacks and a small one, this goes even higher, since free-rolling the third-place player would be disastrous. A hand like A-Ko should usually be folded to a shove in this case, as it has only 65-percent equity against a random hand, and you may still even fold hands that have about the right equity if your opponents may make foolish mistakes and free-roll you later.

This should be your basic game plan throughout Steps 1-5, with slight modifications, depending on the level of your opposition. In the early game you might play more hands at lower steps if you feel you have a big edge or there are many bad players, but at the higher steps you may want to tighten up, as you could encounter excellent players who buy in at that level. Similarly, in the endgame players in the lower buy-in steps will often not understand correct strategy and will do foolish things, meaning that you should be careful about moving all-in against them with marginal hands or making marginal calls, whereas higher-stakes players will rarely call when you shove against them on the bubble.

Once you reach Step 6, you will need to tailor your play to the structure of the tournament. The Monte Carlo Step 6 pays an $18,800 package to first place and $1,200 cash to second place, so you should play to win. The LAPT events play more like the lower steps, with several packages on offer, meaning there will be a tightly fought endgame, and so you should beware of playing all-in on the bubble. Slightly different again are the WSOP Steps, which traditionally offer one $12,000 package and several cash prizes. The cash prizes are spread quite thinly, with none usually worth more than the $2,000 entry, so you should again mostly play to win, but also watch for chances to exploit lower-stakes players who might play too tight and try to win a few hundred dollars more.

Hyper-turbo Sitngos

Hyper-turbo sitngos follow the standard payout structures of full-ring or six-max sitngos, but take the popular turbo format to the extreme, giving players stacks of only 10 big blinds to start with, and quickly increasing levels. Full Tilt Poker has this game in the standard full-ring format. PokerStars offers a satellite, giving players the option to unregister from the target event and pocket the registration fee. Winning depends highly on luck, so you should not expect a high return on investment. Look for very low rakes to compensate. These games can be fun and profitable if you manage to play against weak-tight players or in games with little or no rake.

As regards strategy, you should turn immediately to the push-or-fold style of the late game in normal sitngos. Be prepared to gamble with the intent to accumulate a stack early, as waiting for hands will likely cripple you. Because you are limited on chips and the levels may be shorter than normal, you should pay attention to when the blinds increase and budget for this. Watch for antes, which can make a round very expensive or a shove quite profitable. Finally, because the blinds often get very high, try to figure out which players will be pot-committed in the big blind rather than relying simply on ICM calculations, which become less relevant with high blinds.

Matrix Sitngos

Players in Full Tilt's Matrix sitngos are placed on four separate tables. The buy-in is split five ways, with 20 percent going to prizes in the four simultaneous sitngos and the remainder allocated to the best overall players based on a leaderboard. This is a fun format for anyone wanting to play in a mini-league or with friends. Players can observe how others play at all four tables, even if they've been eliminated from a table.

Matrix sitngos have seen limited popularity so far, and so only tend to run regularly at small buy-ins, typically $24 or below, which when split five ways is equivalent to playing approximately $5 games.

Strategy is mostly the same as in normal sitngos, but leaderboard considerations can alter strategy in marginal situations and at the end of the game, when it is clearer who is still in contention. Players earn one point for each opponent they outlast, two points for every player they knock out at each table and an additional two points if they win at that table, so there is a definite bias toward aggressive play and accumulation of chips in marginal spots. Earned, maximum and projected points are displayed in the sitngo lobby, so you can keep an eye on things and predict the end outcome. You sometimes might want to change your play against an opponent in an attempt to avoid being overtaken.

The maximum leaderboard score on any one table is 26 (two points for knocking out each player plus one for surviving them and two for winning) so your overall maximum score is 104. Getting anywhere near this score is highly unlikely. With the leaderboard money also being paid out on a 50/30.20 basis, 30 points overall should be good enough for a cash, and 40 or more should give you a good shot at winning. If you win all four tables, you will be crowned the Dominatrix and claim all of the leaderboard money (although the chances of this are minute).

Pot-limit Omaha Sitngos

Pot-limit Omaha has consistently grown in popularity over the last few years to the point where it challenges no-limit hold'em as the high-stakes players' game of choice. It is a more complex and sophisticated game, but it also involves more gambling and luck, which keeps weaker players happy. Though the structure is similar to hold'em, many adjustments are required, and sitngos are a good place for beginners to try them out. If you are experienced at sitngo play, the format allows you to employ some profitable strategic adjustments against weaker players.

The structure and hand rankings for pot-limit Omaha are the same as in hold'em, but players are dealt four cards and must use exactly two, whereas in hold'em they can use any number, including none. The pot-limit betting structure limits bets to the amount it takes to call the last bet plus the total money now in play. So, if you are starting with blinds of 10/20 it will cost you 20 to call, and you can raise another 50, so your pot-sized raise will total 70 and the pot will contain 100. If the next player wants to re-raise, he can call 70 and raise as much as 100 + 70 + 70 = 240.

In the early stages of a PLO sitngo, you will be reasonably deep with stacks of 50-75 big blinds. You will need to amass some chips, assuming you are playing the standard format with a 50/30/20 payout. However, since you cannot re-buy and PLO is a game of small edges and high variance, you want to be wary of getting into big pots without a big equity edge. Limping in early position and calling raises is preferable to raising and re-raising liberally, although you should still raise most hands in late position when you can control the pot or steal the blinds.

You want your four cards (six two-card combinations) to work together. Hands like 6-7-8-9 or A-K-Q-T double-suited are very desirable, as are high pairs with strong supporting cards, such as K-K-Q-J or A-A-T-J with suits. Beware of middle or low pairs, which may flop an underset or inhibit your wrap (e.g., 6-7-7-8), dry aces (like A-A-4-8 rainbow), which are easily outdrawn, and other unconnected or weak hands. Of course, on the button or in the cutoff, you can raise much wider, as you will be able to bluff and put your opponent in tough situations.

Post-flop, you want to be drawing to the nuts most of the time and looking to flop very strong hands, since with six combinations, it is much more likely that someone will hit the board hard, and in a multi-way pot if a flush or straight is possible, someone will usually have made it, making it tricky to get involved with weaker or non-nut hands. This enables you to play aggressively in position, continuation-betting and barreling as scare cards come. Your opponent will be hard-pressed to call down without a very strong hand—in pot-limit Omaha even a decent flush is often a bluff-catcher if it's not the nuts or the board pairs. You should play very tight out of position pre-flop to avoid playing marginal hands post-flop, and often re-raise to reduce your positional disadvantage (as the stack-to-pot ratio will now be reduced) and seize the momentum.

Draws are often favorites over made hands in PLO. You may have a set and be flipping or even behind a big wrap with multiple straight or flush outs. Low sets and hands like top two pair are often much weaker than they appear; you should sometimes play them cautiously on the flop and wait for a safe turn card. Similarly, with weaker draws, a bad turn card will often kill your hand; you can get away cheaply if you just called on the flop. If you are new to pot-limit Omaha, you should simulate hands on sites like twodimes.net and propokertools.com to get a feel for the percentages.

As the blinds get higher and players are eliminated, the sitngo format becomes more important because of the same ICM considerations that apply in no-limit hold'em sitngos, where we have seen that you would need to be a decent favorite to get all-in pre-flop in the early going, and a very big favorite to get all-in on the bubble with even stacks (in the latter case about 65 percent or more). However, because pre-flop equities run so close in PLO, it's very hard to be more than a 65-percent favorite with anything less than strong aces, and so you should play cautiously as the game progresses, limping more where getting re-raised is terrible for you and calling raises rather than re-raising even with strong drawing hands.

This is also partly due to the pot-limit format, which makes bubble play far more complicated than in no-limit hold'em, where you can simply move all-in for 10 or even 15 big blinds with many hands. In pot-limit Omaha, only being able to raise to 3.5 big blinds or re-raise a pot-raise to 12 big blinds gives your opponents lots of leverage and will often put you in tough situations, unless you have a shorter stack where you can get most of your chips in pre-flop, in which case you should do so with most decent hands, especially when in last position, since you need to accumulate chips to have a chance.

With a deep stack, it's very important to plan your hand so that you can avoid committing yourself without a big equity edge, which can benefit your opponents considerably. It's also a good idea to limit your pre-flop raises to 2.5 times the pot as the blinds rise. This makes it easier to fold to re-raises, and limits re-raises to nine times the initial pot, so that you can call and see flops much more cheaply.

Planning is particularly important near the bubble, where you can get yourself into trouble with marginal hands because of ICM considerations. You should usually tighten up unless you are the biggest or smallest stack. You can steal the blinds of very tight players or in late position if you are unlikely to land in a bad situation, and it's okay to get all-in with a raise or re-raise if you have a strong hand.

You can play quite aggressively if your stack is so big that you can afford to lose all-ins. In a pot-limit game, people can't easily move all-in against you or re-raise you out of pots. Use this fact to force them to fold after they've put some chips in the pot. With a big lead, your opponents will be reduced to playing for second and third, and you can raise every hand and rarely suffer greatly. Even out of position, you can afford to call raises, and then move all-in on many flops where you have reasonable equity, putting your opponent to the test for his whole stack.

This is where you can show the most profit by far in pot-limit Omaha sitngos. While you shouldn't gamble recklessly early on, you should try to get in pots when you have a big stack (especially against weaker players).

Three-handed and heads-up play require the same adjustments as in hold'em sitngos, with the end of the bubble freeing people up to play more hands unless they are still competing for second with a short stack. Bear this in mind in your opening, calling and re-raising ranges, and be careful not to get anted away. Again, stack sizes are key here, so look for ways to manipulate them so that someone else is likely to make a mistake like raising and then betting any flop all-in when checked to, and above all, play to win unless there is a compelling reason to wait and try to secure second place.

Pot-limit Omaha High-low Sitngos

Pot-limit games have always been popular in the UK and Europe. While hold'em and Omaha have dominated, pot-limit Omaha high-low is one of the few other games to be played with much frequency, whether in mixed games or on its own. It has gained popularity due to online poker. It combines the skill and aggression required to win at big-bet poker with the finesse and balance of split-pot games, which are usually played at fixed limits. Few people play the game well, and it can be particularly profitable in a sitngo format where many players are new to both the game and the sitngo structure, especially when buy-ins for online sitngos regularly run up to $200.

The rules are the same as in PLO, but you make both a high and a low hand, using any two of your four cards for each. High hand rankings are standard, but a low must consist of five differently ranked cards, ace to eight, with the lowest five cards winning. The best hand is A-2-3-4-5, called a wheel.

Because a hand must consist of two hole cards and three community cards, a low is only possible when there are three low cards on the board. The high hand scoops the whole pot if there is no low (though one player can win both high and low). Because players usually play hands including A-2 or A-3, the low part of the pot will often be split, so besides scooping or winning half in any given hand, you might get quartered if you tie for low and have a losing high hand, or you can win 3/4 of the pot if you win high and tie for low.

The winning low hand has the lowest top card. For example, A-2-3-4-5 beats A-2-3-4-6, and 2-3-4-5-7 beats A-2-3-4-8. You can usually determine the nut low by identifying the lowest two vacant slots on the board (assuming a low is possible). For example, A-2-3-4-5 is the nut low on a board of A-3-4-K-Q. An exception occurs when there are four cards to a wheel on the board, so on a board of A-3-4-5-Q any player with a deuce and another wheel card has the nut low.

Your goal in any split-pot game is to win both ends, since winning only half the pot will rarely give you a significant profit. This is particularly important in a pot-limit game. Players can find themselves being free-rolled by a hand with a lock on one side of the pot and outs to the other for all of their chips. It is essential to play hands with good potential in both directions, and usually at least one nut draw.

The best hand is A-A-2-3 double-suited, which has the best pair and draws, as well as an extra low card to protect from being counterfeited for the low if an ace, deuce or three fall, as the other two cards will still play. In contrast, if you have A-A-2-K, an ace or deuce can ruin your chances of winning the low, as one of your cards is dead. You will seldom see hands this strong, but most hands with A-2 and other low cards, nut-flush draws and high cards like A-2-K-Q, A-A-3-K and A-3-4-6 are all very playable, and you can add more hands when you are in late position.

High-only hands like A-A-K-K or A-K-Q-J are playable, but with no chance for low, you will want to see cheap flops that contain high cards, making a low hand unlikely, and make players pay the maximum to chase low draws.

Deeper-stacked play is very much determined by the flop, which may make a strong hand worthless if it doesn't connect, is counterfeited or is drawing in only one direction. Similarly, getting all-in pre-flop with hands weaker than a big pair and a good low is rarely a good idea, since something like A-2-3-4 or A-A-K-Q can perform pretty poorly against a hand with two-way potential. Avoid putting too many chips in before the flop with speculative or one-way hands. See where you stand before committing.

Because this is big-bet poker, you will usually want to play aggressively after the flop if you have a lock hand with outs in another direction, such as the nut low and a flush draw or a strong high hand with nut-low outs. You want to force other players out or make them pay to chase half the pot. Avoid building big pots if you only have something like a nut low with no redraws or counterfeit protection, as another player will often have the same low with high outs or backup for the low.

Because of this dynamic, position is key. With position, you can force someone into bad situations such as calling down with a non-nut hand for half the pot on later streets, or you can bet big on the river in the hope of folding out one of these hands. In multi-way pots, you may have to fold a hand like the nut low with no high draws if there is a lot of action post-flop, the stacks are deep and there is not a lot of money yet in the pot, since you will often get 1/4 of the pot back, or less.

As the game becomes more short-handed and the blinds go up, you will be more likely to get all-in pre-flop or on the flop, and so you need to be careful about selecting hands and committing your stack in marginal spots. Look to see a flop unless your hand is very strong in both directions, and then put your money in, which may force an opponent with a marginal hand to fold.

If you are on or near the bubble with a medium stack, the same considerations apply as in pot-limit Omaha. Your stack size is paramount, both in terms of your overall position and the number of big blinds you have. Because you can only raise to 3.5 times the pot, you need to be extremely careful with a deeper stack, as you will often commit yourself to call a re-raise before the flop or to go all-in on the flop. Be very selective about when you raise and whom you raise, because an aggressive big stack can put you in very bad situations. If you have only seven big blinds, you should raise only with good two-way potential, and counterfeit protection if possible, in which case you are usually happy to bet your remaining chips post-flop. With 10-12 big blinds, consider raising only to 2.5 times the big blind, so that you can comfortably fold to a re-raise..

With the big stack, you can wreak havoc on the bubble. Your raise will often commit you to calling a re-raise or all-in, and you will often chop the pot and still have a big stack. Look for opportunities to force other players out of pots, either by a re-raise when they are not pot-committed or with a "stop and go" play in which you call pre-flop and bet favorable flops that they might have missed. You have massive leverage with a big stack because of the closeness of hand equities in this game, and because it is tough to scoop.

When the bubble bursts, you can start to gamble for first place with a short or medium stack. Here and in heads-up play, you must widen your hand ranges significantly. Anything with moderate two-way potential or good one-way potential will now warrant a raise, since you can often pick up the blinds or split the pot.

You can raise many hands when heads-up with position for the same reason, and also because you can use your leverage post-flop some of the time.

Whatever you do, it is particularly important in pot-limit Omaha high-low to plan your hand so as to avoid tough situations, or to exploit your opponents. As long as you focus on this, you should be successful.

Fixed-limit Sitngos

Most sites offer fixed-limit sitngos based on various games including hold'em, stud or draw. We will discuss fixed-limit sitngo play in general and them move on to individual games, including those that make up the H.O.R.S.E. rotation and triple draw, looking at general strategies for each game. We will then consider mixed-game sitngos like H.O.R.S.E. and 8-game.

Strategies for fixed-limit sitngos are fairly straightforward, since you will rarely face the threat of an all-in, and you can control the number of chips you put in the pot until you get very low. For example, in limit hold'em, calling a raise in the big blind and then calling bets on all streets will only cost you three big bets, and so you already know the maximum price of showing down a hand and what effect losing might have on your stack and overall position. Even if you are playing aggressively and run into another aggressive player, most hands are unlikely to cost you more than five big bets. With an extra street, stud games are slightly more expensive, but a similar dynamic applies.

The main questions in fixed-limit sitngos are how to play when you cannot move all your chips in, how to play with a short stack and how to play with a big stack when other players are under pressure. Although there will be fewer all-ins in these formats, ICM considerations still apply.

You should generally play more conservatively than in a cash game. This may mean putting in less action pre-flop or on third street with marginal hands (or just folding them), but also making less risky call-downs if losing can threaten your overall position. Even if you do not get all-in, you can rarely afford to lose more than two or three big pots in succession once the blinds are high, so you should choose your spots carefully to yield the best expectation.

When very short-stacked, try to play hands with good implied odds, such as big cards and pairs in hold'em, and avoid hands like suited connectors or small pairs that can land you in tricky spots and that you may have to fold before putting your last chips in. This won't matter much when you're so short that you can get most of your chips in early in a hand.

Conversely, you can play more loosely with a big stack, since most players will play tighter than in a cash game and tend towards a fit-or-fold strategy post-flop. This gives you excellent odds on your pre-flop steals and your flop continuation bets in limit hold'em and on third and fourth street bets in stud games. In limit hold'em, for example, you are risking two small bets to win 1.5 pre-flop, and if called by only the big blind, one small bet to win 4.5 small bets on the flop.

Mixed-game and fixed-limit sitngos are certainly less popular that pot- and no-limit varieties (although games do run in some formats up to the $200 level), but they are more profitable at the lower buy-ins that single-game sitngos. These sitngos are an excellent way to learn other games cheaply against weak players, since you play a lot for a small sum.

Limit Hold'em Sitngos

General Strategy

Limit hold'em requires very different strategies than big-bet players are used to. This is mainly due to the betting structure, which has two rounds of smaller bets followed by two rounds of double bets. So if a sitngo starts with 20/40 limits the blinds would be 10 and 20, with bets of 20 pre- and post-flop and bets of 40 on the turn and river (with a maximum four bets per round).

To win at limit hold'em, you must play a more straightforward game, at least at a full table. This starts with fairly strict starting hand requirements, so in early position (the first three seats after the blinds at a nine-handed table), you should mainly play big aces, pairs and connectors (A-Jo+, A-10s+, K-Js+, 8-8+) as well as occasional mix-up hands like lower suited connectors, and raise to thin the field.

A few more aces become playable in middle position (the next two seats), along with more pairs and connectors, so your range might now be all suited aces,

A-8o+, 6-6+ and a variety of middle to high Broadway and suited connectors, depending on the game.

You can open much wider in late position (the cutoff and button) since you stand to steal the blinds or get heads-up in position more often. Most pairs and aces are playable, though you might sometimes fold ace-rag, 2-2 and 3-3 in the cutoff. You can raise with more connected and suited hands in the cutoff and a very wide range from the button, including hands like 8-9o, Q-6s, K-5s and A-2o. Remember that because limit hold'em is a game of showdowns, you should avoid most unsuited hands with cards below a 6. These cards usually have reverse implied odds because pairing them will put you in tough situations.

If an earlier player enters with a limp or a raise, you should generally raise or reraise if you're playing. This helps you to isolate and take momentum. You may elect to just call with a speculative hand like a small pair or suited connectors if several players have limped or cold-called in front of you.

When you have been re-raised, you will have the option of calling or capping. The most important considerations are value, position and deception. If you have position, the re-raiser will almost always bet the flop if you call, so you'll get the extra bet anyway, and can deceive your opponent if you have a strong hand like aces. Out of position with that strong hand, you may wish to cap so that you get maximum value. You should sometimes cap lightly in or out of position with hands like suited connectors against an aggressive opponent to counter his strategy and deceive him.

In the big blind, you can often call for a single bet with excellent pot odds, and it will be cheaper for you to get to showdown than in no-limit hold'em. For example, with 20/40 blinds, if the button raises your big blind and the small blind folds, then you will get 70-to-20 odds to call, and since a raiser invariably bets the flop when checked to, it's more like 90-to-20. Then it will only cost you a maximum of another 100 chips to showdown if your opponent bets every street, giving you odds of 190-to-100. Getting almost 2-to-1 odds from start to finish, you should defend with a wide variety of hands and often call down with any part of the board or ace-high. You should still not defend with low unsuited hands like 9-3 or 10-2.

The raiser's position makes a huge difference. You should usually abandon weak, unsuited aces against a tight player in early position, but these hands are often playable against late-position raisers, as are most suited, connected or middle-high cards. Finally, you can defend almost any hand in the big blind if the small blind raises, since you will have position. Being heads-up in the small blind is also interesting, and against a player who usually defends his big blind, to a raise you may consider limping some of your weaker hands to prevent building a pot out of position with a weak hand and little fold equity.

You can also respond to a raise with a re-raise in the big blind. Because you will have so many weak hands in your range, it's usually best to just call an early- or middle-position raiser, although you may elect to re-raise an aggressive late-position player. Almost all players will bet the flop when you check, so again, if you just call the pre-flop raise, you'll get that extra bet when you want it, and with hands like middle pairs, it will allow you to see a safe flop before you put more chips in the pot, and will also disguise your hand.

Post-Flop Play

Although limit hold'em is mainly a pre-flop game, play after the flop is crucial to winning, as you often face close decisions on three streets. On the flop, it is almost automatic for the pre-flop aggressor to fire a continuation bet (unless there are several players in the hand). The bets don't double until the turn, so you should often call on the flop with as little as a low pair, a gutshot, overcards or backdoor outs if there are a lot of bets in the pot and you are closing the action.

If you are the aggressor, you should almost always bet the flop if you have narrowed the opposition to one or two players, or if you have a decent hand or draw, hoping to win immediately. Many players call lightly on the flop, so you should often fire the turn as well. In limit hold'em, one pair is a strong hand. Players often miss, and you are getting good odds to call down or improve, so you should be very tenacious with such hands and not fold unless you are clearly losing. Similarly, you should often call down the whole way with ace-high against aggressive players, folding on the river only if you don't think your opponent would bluff three streets, or if the main draws on the board were completed.

Similarly, with a strong or moderate made hand or a draw, you should bet relentlessly, expect to be called down lightly and slow down only when you are raised and you have a marginal hand. Players usually raise on the flop or turn. Some will take the board and your hand strength into account. You must decide how to respond, based on their tendencies.

Players will generally check-raise on the flop with a wide variety of hands, including pairs, draws, overcards and stronger hands. If they wait until the turn, they often have a strong hand and want to win an extra big bet instead of a small one.

This should also be your general strategy, although raising the turn as a bluff or semi-bluff is also a very powerful strategy. If you are check-raised as the aggressor and you have a strong hand, you can three-bet the flop, or call the raise and then raise the turn. The same principles apply, although with a strong hand on a semi-coordinated flop you may wish to jam and disguise your hand strength rather than risk looking like you are trapping. If you are out of position with a strong hand and face a raise, then you should usually three-bet, as some players will raise to take a free card on the next street and this would be a disaster.

You will often find yourself on the river with a marginal hand. If you are the aggressor, then you should bet most made hands for value unless the board is very scary, as you can be called by as little as ace-high. You should rarely fold to a bet because the pot is large and you are getting excellent odds. However, hand reading is important, and you will often be able to fold ace-high or a low pair because all the draws got there or you do not expect your opponent to three-barrel.

Limit Hold'em Sitngo Adjustments

We have presented a basic strategy for limit hold'em games whose players have a reasonable understanding of the game. You may have to alter your strategy slightly for sitngos because you can't re-buy, and also against opponents who are not familiar with the loose and aggressive play of the limit game. In the early stages when there is no chip pressure, you can play aggressively to build a stack if your opponents give up too easily, and then bully them when the bubble approaches and they are under chip pressure.

You should play much tighter early if you get short-stacked, and also if you are one of the lower stacks near the bubble. Try to limit your play to big cards and big pairs that play well post-flop, unless you can attack very tight players in late position. This will also be key when it comes to spending your last few chips. Try not to put a significant proportion of your stack in before the flop if you may be forced to fold on the flop, knocking you down even further.

Limit Omaha High-low Sitngos

General Strategy

Omaha high-low is popular at fixed limits, particularly in the U.S. Your strategy should combine the starting hand concepts of Pot-limit Omaha high-low with some limit hold'em theory.

Look for hands that can win both ways, with nut outs in at least one direction. Any A-2 is usually playable, as is an A-3 with a nut-flush draw and weaker lows with counterfeit protection or high potential. Also good are hands with very strong high potential and a low draw, such as A-A-x-x or A-K-Q-4 double-suited. Low wrap hands with three or four cards to a wheel (including an ace) are also very strong, as they are seldom counterfeited for low, and often make straights as well.

You can play somewhat looser than at pot-limit because it's easier to get to show-down and far less expensive to risk being free-rolled for half the pot if your opponent bets every street. Getting quartered is rarely a big threat, since the pot will usually be laying you the right price to call. As in limit hold'em, you can call much more liberally in the big blind, and even more so, since it is very difficult for your opponent to scoop.

Therefore, you can defend a wide range of hands, provided they have reasonable potential both ways or good potential in one. Similarly, peeling the flop with backdoor draws is even more prevalent here since you will often pick up outs on the turn. Paradoxically, you should be more inclined to play marginal holdings in the big blind against a single player because you're not too likely to be scooped and you can't be forced to fold by other players' betting and raising.

In late position, you can raise many weaker hands if they have some value, in the expectation of facing only the blinds; hands with many low cards like 2-3-5-6 are now playable, as are weaker aces and high-only hands. You should still avoid hands with a lot of middle cards either in late position or in the blinds. Hands like 6-7-8-9 and 7-7-8-8 will rarely scoop because the cards that help them will usually make someone a low hand.

High hands are quite vulnerable because they cannot force low draws and other high draws out of the pot as in pot-limit, and they risk losing half the pot to a low. You should only play these hands in position, in cheap multi-way pots or out of the big blind, and continue only on a very favorable high flop.

Only an absolutely premium high hand will be profitable in most cases, which generally means four Broadway cards with a suited ace, or aces with high suited kickers. Drawing to king- and queen-high flushes is expensive in this game, since your opponents will often play suited aces, and if you have a lower wrap like 8-9-10-J, some of your straight outs help make a low, so can expect to win no more than half the pot. You may defend high hands in the big blind more liberally due to pot odds, but be prepared to get away quickly if you don't flop a big hand or draw.

Whether to call or raise pre-flop depends on whether you wish to play multi-way or thin the field. For example, a weak A-2 hand may have limited value in a raised pot, but by limping in, you may invite other players in that may add value to your low, such as those holding A-3 or A-4 hands. Limping is therefore quite viable in early position, but in late position you should still raise most hands you intend to play, at least when you open the betting.

Raising before the flop has unique advantages in this game. First, winning the blinds is excellent, as so many pots are split. It also makes you harder to read than a player who only raises with A-A or A-2 hands. Finally, it helps you to narrow your opponents' holdings. For example, if you raise with A-A-3-4 and the flop comes 9-9-2, you can be fairly sure your hand is best for high against competent opponents.

When there are already limpers or raisers in a pot, you can again decide whether to raise or cold-call based on your hand.

Post-Flop Play

As we discussed earlier, the flop can make an average hand or break a great one. However, because the flop coincides with the second small betting round, you should rarely fold unless your hand has completely missed or is counterfeited. You should aim for the nuts in one direction and have a shot in the other, but the odds on the flop may justify your taking a card with nothing but good backdoor draws. You should still generally make a continuation bet if you're the aggressor, and with the bloated pot you will often peel to a check-raise.

Turn and river play follow a similar pattern, but by now you should have a fair idea of your prospects. The bet size doubles on the turn, so you need a reasonable hand or a draw in at least one direction to continue, and you will need to assess how the turn card has helped any backdoor draws you had on the flop. If you are the aggressor, you should not expect opponents to fold on the turn as often as they do in limit hold'em, since many draws and backdoors are possible, and so you should bet for value more often and be prepared to check in situations where you would hate getting check-raised or you only have a bare draw in one direction.

Pay attention to what draws develop, and whether the low comes in. Try to match this information to your opponents' hand ranges to determine your move. Aggressive play with only the nut low in a multi-way pot is rarely a good idea, as you risk being quartered or worse. But you shouldn't mind escalating the betting with a strong two-way draw, or if you have the nut low and counterfeit protection or a reasonable chance at the high.

Hand reading is easier in limit Omaha high-low than in other games because people play more straightforwardly. If a solid player leads into the field on a high-only board, he probably has the nuts or close to it, and similarly, he will usually have the nuts with additional outs if he escalates the betting when the low is out. Just get out of the way and wait for your turn to come. However, players will often bet a good low draw the whole way in a heads-up situation, and bluff the river if they miss. In this case you can call down light.

Sitngo Adjustments

You should take a slightly different approach than in a cash game for a fixed-limit Omaha high-low sitngo.

Aggressive play can work well in the early game if your opponents are overly tight, and is an excellent strategy when you have the chip lead near to the bubble.

Once you are short-stacked, you need to adjust. Omaha high-low is a game of hitting flops. If you think you will be unable to steal the blinds often, you may consider limping, which can enable you to put a lot of chips in when you hit and get away cheaply when you miss. This will maximize your opportunities to rebuild. You will hit a lot of flops with a two-way hand. Once you have something reasonable, you can try to force other players out or gain value for your hand, since even if you don't scoop, you will usually win at least half the pot.

Razz Sitngos

General Rules and Strategy

Razz is a low-only stud game with up to eight players. Each player posts an ante before each hand and receives three cards, two down (which are hole cards, as in hold'em) and one up. This is called "third street". The first betting round takes place, followed by three more up-cards (fourth, fifth and sixth street), each with its own betting round, and then a final down-card (seventh street) and betting round. The highest exposed card on third street must post a bring-in, with the option to raise. There are five betting rounds, with betting increments doubling on fifth street.

In a razz sitngo with betting limits of 10/20, everyone might post an ante of 2 and the highest card might post a bring-in of 4 or raise to 10. After this, betting proceeds clockwise, with players being able to call the bring-in or raise in appropriate increments; at 10/20 this would be 10 for the first two streets, and 20 from fifth street through seventh street, with a maximum of four bets per street.

The aim of the game is straightforward: you must make the lowest five-card hand, the nuts being A-2-3-4-5 (known as a wheel) and all other hands being ranked from the top down, with A-2-4-5-7 beating A-2-3-6-7, for example, because while tied with 7, the first hand's 5 beats the second hand's 6. Traditional poker hands are irrelevant in razz. You simply play your best five cards, with aces always playing low.

Razz is the most straightforward of the mixed games, with a player's hand rarely being well disguised and the victor in any given confrontation often being determined by luck as much as anything. However, the game still involves considerable skill, and most players aren't aware of a few interesting situations that can arise.

The first thing to consider is the effect of the high card having to start the action. The opener is doomed unless he has a small card. If everyone folds to you in last position, you should almost always raise and expect a fold, even if you have something like 8-8-(8) against a Jack. If he calls (which either means he is a weak player or he has something like A-2 in the hole), you can still win by catching good on the next card and betting.

You should usually steal through one low card (eight or below), and sometimes through two such players when the pot is large due to the ante size or the number of players and you show a good low card. If you steal with a bad hole card and are re-raised, you should give up unless you suspect a re-steal. You should usually fold to a raise with a high card in the bring-in unless you have two undercards to the raiser's up-card, suspect a steal and will be heads-up.

If you are in early position relative to the bring-in, you must consider not only your hand, but which of your cards is visible and what your opponents are showing.

The latter exercise tells you how likely you are to have the best hand, and whether any of the cards you need are dead.

For example, if you are dealt A-4-8 in early position, there is usually a significant difference between having the eight and the ace exposed. If everyone else shows a high card, then you should raise and expect to win the hand (even without such good hole cards). But if you raise when a couple of players are showing cards lower than yours, they will fear you much less than if you showed an ace. Showing an 8, you will have to proceed with caution because you may not know if bets on later streets are for value or deception.

It might be best to muck your hand if many low cards are out, as you are unlikely to be best, especially if the cards showing are ones you need. If there are two fours, two aces and an eight showing and your ace is up, then you would certainly want to raise because your hand is very live. But if your four or eight is up and there are many twos, threes, fives, sixes or sevens showing, then you would have a clear fold.

Depending on the ante structure, you might also limp with some marginal hands to test the water, since there is little pure bluffing in razz. In the above example, if your hand is very live, but the eight is up and there are aces and fours showing, then you might just limp and try to see fourth street cheaply, since other players will have a fair idea of your hand range. If you are going to do this with any regularity, then you should conceal the strength of your hand by sometimes limping with strong hands and raising with weak ones. Open-raising is usually the best option, especially with antes greater than 1/10 of the big bet, in which case winning the dead money will add significantly to your stack.

You should usually play only strong low hands (mainly three cards eight or lower) on third street, but adjust your play based on your opponents' up-cards. You should also use this information when deciding whether to flat-call or re-raise. In a re-raised pot, you should call on fourth street with any decent hand, even if you catch bad and your opponent catches good, but this is often a significant error in a single-raised pot.

Try to manipulate the pot size to your advantage, based on your hand and your opponents' tendencies. For example, if a player raises in a steal position, you should always re-raise a strong hand to avoid incorrectly folding on fourth street, but you should just call with a marginal hand to an early-position raise, allowing yourself to get away cheaply on later streets. Similarly, some bad opponents will peel too lightly on fourth street, and against them you should be more inclined to flat-call since you will often be able to get away on fourth street correctly but they will not.

The Later Streets

Play on the later streets is mostly determined by the new up-cards that are dealt, with the lowest hand on the board acting first and almost always choosing to bet and represent the best hand overall. As you can see, this leaves little room for finesse, and so the issue is often whether to continue when you fall behind, and whether your opponent could have paired a hole card or might be betting on the fact that you caught bad.

We have seen that in a re-raised pot, you should take a card on fourth street for a single small bet if you catch bad and your opponent catches good. You should also consider calling if you started with a very strong hand and your opponent catches marginally good. Otherwise you should fold. Regardless, you must improve to a potentially winning draw by fifth street, when the bets double, if you are to continue calling down. Even A-2-3 is junk if it catches two paired or high cards, unless your opponent has also caught bad twice.

For example if you re-raised with a very live A-2-3 and were called by an eight which caught a seven on fourth street to your king, you would certainly call a bet and chase all the way if you caught a 4, 5, 6, 7 or 8 on fifth street (but fold otherwise). This is because in razz, you can always determine your opponent's best possible hand. If you both caught low cards on fifth street, with you making a wheel draw, then your A-2-3-4-K would have an ample chance to improve against his best possible holding of A-2-3-7-8.

Fifth street is the key point in razz due to the bets doubling. Once you call here, you are often committed to going all the way unless your opponent catches extremely strong cards and it becomes likely that even making your draw will not guarantee victory. It is also an interesting pivotal point in the battle between draws and made hands, as a bad nine is actually losing to a strong draw such as A-2-3-4-K, with A-2-3-8-9 having only 40-percent equity and A-2-3-7-9 having only about 45-percent equity against this hand. You can win extra bets from players who don't know this.

Sixth street is fairly routine in razz unless your opponent catches a very good card and you catch bad. The best hand showing will usually continue betting, with the weaker one trying to catch up. Watch for players that give away that they have paired by checking a street when they have a strong board, or who check-raise if you bet with a reasonably strong board.

Seventh street is more interesting, as it is dealt face-down. Pay close attention to the boards of players still in the hand. These, combined with their prior actions, can provide much information about their possible holdings. The pot is usually so big that you should call even if there is only a slight chance you can win. You should often call a bet in the hope that your opponent has paired or double-paired along the way, or started with a bad card from a steal position. You can also bet thinly for value in many spots, especially when you have strong low cards showing. You will rarely be raised, since you can have the nuts or close to it.

Consider the up-cards and your opponent's actions when deciding if he might have paired. For example, a player betting aggressively on third street who catches a 7 or 8 is unlikely to have paired. In our initial example, when an 8 limps, if the player is observant, it should be possible to infer that he holds some of the cards that are dead and play accordingly on future streets.

Sitngo Strategy

Sitngo stud games are unusual in that without very large blinds to force the action, players can often survive for a long time. If you start with 1,500 chips, the limits might have reached 150/300, giving you only five big bets, but the ante would usually be 30 or less, with a bring-in of perhaps 60. Unless you are unlucky and get several successive bring-ins, you can survive without taking action for 20-30 hands.

When the limits get very high, you should avoid playing marginal hands that can cost you a large part of your stack, unless you have a good steal opportunity. Wait for a good starting hand and play it according to your stack size and hand strength. With a very short stack and a strong hand, you should play aggressively straight away, since you will be able to get most of your money in on third street. With a slightly deeper stack and a more marginal hand, you may opt to limp or call a raise and be sure to have caught another low card by fifth street, at which point you can happily get the rest of your money in.

Seven-card Stud Sitngos

The rules of seven-card stud are similar to those of razz, except that it is a high-only game in which players must use five of their seven cards to make a hand. The low card brings it in. A player pairing his door card can make a big bet on fourth street, a quirk not replicated in other stud games.

Hold'em players will need to make some adjustments when selecting starting hands. The value of a starting stud hand depends on your up-card as well as those of other players. Your hand's strength depends on whether the cards that are out are ones that you need to complete a hand, and whether they are higher or lower than your cards. The pot size and your position relative to the bring-in also come into play.

Because players have their own boards, it is much harder to be dominated by another hand, and so hand values run much closer in stud than in games with community cards. We will now look at the major hand groupings and how to play them.

Trips

Three of a kind is a monster stud hand that should always be played. The only problem you will face is how best to get as much money into the pot as possible, which will depend upon your up card. If you have (2-2)-2, then you may want to play cautiously on the early streets to avoid giving your hand away, but if you have (A-A)-A, then you should put in every bet you can, as people will already suspect that you have a strong hand.

High Pairs

These are also quite strong, as it is unlikely that anyone has a better hand, and anytime you pair your kicker you will likely have the best two-pair hand in play. What constitutes a high pair will vary according to the other cards out. For example, (10-8)-10 is probably the best hand if all the other up-cards are lower than a ten. You should play aggressively if you believe you have the best pair, by raising or re-raising to limit the field and charge draws. Proceed with caution if there are several face cards and aces out, as someone likely has a higher pair.

Low Pair/High Kicker

A low pair with a high kicker is fairly strong because it can improve to beat middle pair, middle kicker. For example, (2-2)-A has around 45-percent equity vs. (10-8)-10 if the ace is suited. You should play a low pair with a high kicker aggressively on third street. This disguises your hand and gives you an additional way to win if you catch a scare card and can force another player to fold.

Low Pair/Low Kicker

Unlike the other pair hands, this one should be played with caution or folded, as it is rarely in good shape. You will often trail a better pair, and when you make two pair, you will often lose to a better two pair. The board cards that are out are important in defining this hand. Your strong (10-8)-10 in the previous section would be much weaker with several face cards or aces out behind you. Your (10-8)-10 would be almost a 2-to-1 dog against (A-A)-2.

Three to a Flush

Three cards to a flush, especially three high cards to a flush or three to a straight flush, are very playable, although you should note the number of your flush cards that are already out. Your hand is very live with at most one of your suit out. With two showing, it becomes very marginal, and with three or more it's almost unplayable without high cards, straight cards or steal potential. With drawing hands, you should still play aggressively to disguise your hand and steal the antes in late position, but you should also be happy to play multi-way pots, maximizing your winnings when you hit.

Three to a Straight

This is an overplayed hand in stud. Play three to a straight with caution or fold unless you have overcards to the other board cards and your pair and straight outs are very live. When you make a straight, you will sometimes lose to a flush or full house. Sometimes you will make two pair, and you want them to be a good two pair. Therefore, a hand like (J-Q)-K is very playable against many low cards, while (7-8)-9 is usually unplayable if there are many high cards out or if some of your straight and pair outs are dead.

Three High Cards

Players often assume a big pair when you raise with a high card up. It is usually fine to raise or re-raise with three high cards, as you will often improve to a high pair with a good kicker, a straight draw or a combination of these. Raise this hand in late position or when you have the highest up-card and overcards to the board, e.g., (Q-K)-A against low cards. If a small card raises in late position, you should re-raise to apply pressure and disguise your hand. You can raise much looser in late position to steal with the highest card remaining and almost any other semi-decent cards, especially with tight players behind. You can raise almost any hand with a significantly better up-card than the bring-in, if just you and he remain.

Fourth Street

On fourth street, you will still be putting small bets in the pot. If you have a hand good enough to play on third street for a small bet, you are likely to continue unless something changes radically.

A player who pairs his door card on fourth street has the option to put in a large bet. This is the most radical change of fortune that can occur on fourth street. You should often fold if your opponent pairs his door card, as he will usually have either trips or two pair. You may continue if you are beating trips, have a live four-card draw or two pair, or if you have a live big pair and suspect he does not have trips.

When you pair your door card, you should usually make the larger bet, but you may opt for the smaller bet if you have a very strong hand and suspect players will fold to a large bet. You can also bet the smaller amount to feign strength.

The other scary cards that you or an opponent can catch are an ace or a straight-flush card, which will often hit your down cards or make your hand appear threatening. If the pot is small, you should often fold a marginal hand like a small or medium pair if your opponent catches good and you catch bad, especially if he now has two overcards to your pair and kicker or you have no overcards to his board. On the other hand, if you catch a scary card that does not help you, betting may win the pot or set up a bluff on a later street if your opponent catches bad.

You might slow-play or check-raise a powerful but well-disguised hand like a buried high pair if your opponent has caught a strong-looking card, as this can cause players to misread your hand or win you extra bets. Again, act according to the strength of your board cards and realize that your opponent may take a free card on fifth street if you check and call (so pay attention to who is likely to act first). If you limped in on third street with a strong hand like low trips and nobody raised, you can slow-play and hope to catch the other players out on a later street.

With a decent but vulnerable hand, you should try to knock out players on later streets. You can attempt this either by betting in the hope that the next player will raise, or by checking to a player who you think will bet, and then raising. You may win more money with additional players in the pot, but heads-up, you stand less chance of being outdrawn and may win the pot with only one high pair or two low pair, or even force a single opponent to fold later in the hand.

Fifth Street

The bets double on fifth street. This is a key decision point, since calling often commits you to going to seventh street at a cost of two or more big bets. To continue, you need a hand that either is a likely winner or has a good chance to become one. You will happily call down with a small pair and overcard kickers against a suspected big pair. You will fold without the kickers to hit, or if your opponent has a very scary board and might beat two pair. If you want to continue with a marginal hand, you must ensure that you're drawing for live cards.

If you have been aggressive so far and have a reasonably scary board, you should usually try to force your opponent to fold by betting if he has caught bad. Continue to knock players out if possible to get heads-up, especially if you think you can force someone to fold a slightly better hand or a draw and you have the pot odds to play against the original bettor. You should not be too aggressive with marginal hands against scary boards, as the other player will usually bet for you anyway, and will rarely fold. Don't try to check-raise unless you know that your opponent will often bet when you check.

Sixth Street

The pot is usually sizable by sixth street. Assuming you have some kind of hand, you should have the odds to chase if you are behind, and only fold if your opponent now catches a very scary card. Your options will typically be to bet, check-call or check-raise if you are first to act, and to check, call or raise if your opponent acts first.

When you are heads-up and first to act, you should bet if you think you are ahead or believe your opponent might fold. Check-calling is best if you're less sure, as your opponent will usually bet and you will avoid being raised. Only attempt a check-raise if you are very sure that your opponent will bet a worse hand, but consider it if he might fold to this show of strength, but would call a single bet.

If your opponent acts first and you're heads-up, you should bet your strong and medium-strength hands if checked to and raise very strong hands when your opponent bets. The first player to act will also act first on seventh street, as the boards stay the same, giving you the opportunity to raise for a free card and check the river if you don't improve. You should do this only when you have a hand with good equity, such as a pair and a strong draw, as it will cost you a bet when your opponent might have checked the river anyway, and you may get three-bet.

Seventh Street

You are dealt a down-card on seventh street. You don't know if your opponents have improved, making your decisions more reliant on guesswork and your opinion of your opponents.

When heads-up and first to act, you should usually bet strong hands (two pair or better). You can also bet with a hand like one big pair if you believe your opponent will call with a smaller pair, typically when your pair is concealed, your board is draw-heavy or he is quite loose. Bluff with a busted draw if you bet most of the way and there is a reasonable chance that your opponent will fold.

Check and call if your foe will bet for value but fold a losing pair. Check-raise when you do not have the lead, have improved to a well-disguised hand (like concealed trips) and believe your opponent will bet. You might also check-raise if he is aggressive and value-bets thinly.

When your opponent acts first in a heads-up situation, you should rarely fold for one more bet unless you are sure you are beat or your opponent has a dry board and is unlikely to be bluffing. Raise only when you're fairly sure you have the best hand and your opponent will likely pay you off. You risk a re-raise by a better hand, and worse hands will sometimes fold. Bluff-raise only against a player who value-bets thinly and is capable of folding to a raise.

Value-bet liberally with strong and medium-strength hands when your opponent checks to you. This can include one big pair or two small pair if your opponent is likely to pay you off with worse, but beware the check-raise. You should rarely bluff here, as your opponent will usually check-call with better hands because of the size of the pot, or fold when you are ahead, but you may still fire with a missed draw if your board is scary and your opponent may also have been drawing.

Multi-way, you should only value-bet strong or well-disguised medium-strength hands, and rarely bluff, as someone will typically call. You can again think about raising or check-raising to knock out players who are beating you. With a marginal hand, you should think about whether you are closing the action when faced with a bet, as you may need to call additional bets to showdown. Here you should fold marginal hands if you are quite sure you are not winning.

Sitngo Strategy

Because hand values run close together in stud and it isn't clear from the start exactly what a player has, you can afford to play aggressively early in a stud sitngo and run the table over, particularly since sitngo and tournament formats tend to have a high ante of a tenth of the big bet. As in other formats, if this works, then you will have a good foundation for dominating the bubble and winning the sitngo, particularly since players tend to tighten up in the late stages and wait for good hands rather than risk losing everything on one marginal play.

Wait for good hands with a short stack rather than risk everything on a marginal holding. We have seen several categories of stud hands that are very strong and that you can usually take to the river. While you would love to be dealt trips in such a situation, middle and larger pairs or small pairs with big kickers are usually adequate. Beware of playing speculative stud hands with a short stack, since flush draws, straight draws and high cards can easily brick off, leaving you on the rail. If you can limp or steal with them however, feel free to do so.

Stud High-low Sitngos

In Stud high-low, each player tries to use any five of his seven cards to make high and low hands (it can be a different five for each). High hands are judged according to standard rankings and the low hands must consist of five differently valued cards eight or below, the best low hand being A-2-3-4-5, with standard poker rankings not mattering. Low hands are valued from the top down, so an 8-6 low beats an 8-7 low, for example.

It is important to play hands that can win both halves of the pot. Winning only half will rarely show a large profit, and an opponent might have a lock on one side of the pot and a chance to win your half as well. Furthermore, this game has an extra round of big bets compared to Omaha high-low, giving you worse odds to call down for half the pot. Of course, you can scoop by winning the high side with a hand like a big pair against a low draw that misses, but we will see that is less easy to accomplish.

The golden rule of stud high-low is to play strong starting hands almost all of the time, even when defending or attacking the bring-in; with the low card posting the bring-in, the player opening the action could be sitting on a monster. You generally want to start with three cards to a low, the strongest hands being those with the lowest cards, the most straight or flush potential or an ace that might pair and be good for high (of course being live is also key). Hands like A♥-A♣-2♥ and A♠-2♠-3♠ are among the best (although trips are obviously great), and you can usually play much worse hands.

The main criteria for selecting a starting hand are its potential in either direction, and how the up-cards affect you. For example, you would best fold (2♠-5♥)-8♦ in early position unless almost no low were cards out, and even with the deuce up, still fold against a lot of low up-cards rather than play and risk being scooped. You might play it as a straight steal in late position, since it has little high potential (known in the game as a "razz hand").

You might play a slightly better low hand, like (7♣-6♠)-5♠, even with a lot of low cards out, since you are much more likely to make a straight or flush, and the exposed 5 makes your hand look stronger than it is for the low.

There are a few other playable categories of hands. Three-flushes with at least two low cards are strong hands if not too many flush cards are dead. Paired hands with two low cards are sometimes playable, but you want to have the best pair unless you face just a live high pair. So, (7-7)-2 is much better than (7-2)-2 against other low up-cards, but may still be folded if you face high pairs and legitimate low draws, since you will find it tough to make a hand that can go past fifth street. However, most low paired hands can be defended in the bring-in to a single raise, since you will usually close the action getting good odds. Trips are a monster hand, but should be played in the context of the game, so you could bet and raise early with (2-2)-2 without giving the game away, but would need to trap with (T-T)-T by playing it slower from the start.

High-only hands are much trickier to play, and tend to do better when disguised as low hands, such as (A-K)-A or (K-K)-6. Everyone will know that (6-K)-K, for example, is a high-only hand. They will be able to play perfectly against you, whereas you will be in the dark and sometimes risk getting scooped, or will face tough decisions during the play of the hand. With these hands, you hope to scoop against low draws; try to get heads-up, or play them cheaply and get out early if bad cards come.

When deciding how to play third street, consider the strength of your up-card, whether you want to play heads-up or multi-way, and whether to bloat the pot to make calling on fourth street correct, or to keep it small so you can get away.

The Later Streets

The high-low element makes the later streets more interesting than in other stud games, often allowing good players to take advantage of their less-experienced opponents. High and low hands will often face off, and the way the cards fall on fourth and fifth street before the bets double is key in this battle.

For example, (K-6)-K-6-2 might look good, but it is in mortal danger of being scooped by a hand like (2♠-5♥)-6♠-7♠-4♠. However, should the low hand catch bad, making something like (2♠-5♥)-6♠-10♦-9♥, it can only fold, and even if it catches one low card and gets to (2♠-5♥)-6♠-10♦-8♥, it is still in an awkward spot, usually chasing for just half the pot.

Two apparent low hands will often face off. Again, the next two cards are crucial, as fifth street is crunch time. You should usually fold in a small pot if you catch bad on fourth street against someone who catches good. If the pot is large, or if your starting hand was very strong and your opponent has caught only a marginally good hand, then you can peel and hope for a very strong hand. Fifth street is the time to fold if your hand is still only three to a low or four to a bad low against a scary board. Once you call on fifth street, you are usually going all the way due to the pot size.

Play on sixth street is fairly standard, with the dominant hand usually betting and the weaker hand committed to calling. Don't get carried away with an apparently impregnable high hand against an obvious made low that could still have scoop outs. Putting in four bets with quads is no fun when you lose to a low straight flush.

Seventh street is again interesting, as the cards are dealt face-down. Bet and raise with a lock on either side of the pot, even if your chance of scooping is small. Otherwise, just call unless your scoop potential is high. Almost always call with a marginal hand in the hope of winning half the pot, even if you have a busted low draw that only caught a bad pair on the river against an apparent low hand, unless the pot is very small or your opponent is very likely to have a larger pair. Folding any sort of winning hand at this stage is a massive mistake, especially when your opponent likely has five cards for a low hand, making it less likely for him to have a winning pair.

Sitngo Strategy

Stud high-low is different from other stud games. Because the bring-in is the low card, the opener already has one-third of a strong starting hand. For this reason, and because the high-low element makes more hands playable on third street, it is not such a good idea to play aggressively early and try to accumulate chips. Play a solid game. When the bets double on fifth street, punish those who play weak razz hands for low or overplay high pairs. If by doing this you build a big stack, you can open up somewhat as you approach the bubble.

If you end up short-stacked, as is likely in this format, wait for strong starting hands and play them aggressively. High pairs gain value in this case, since you will be all-in early with no reverse implied odds. Play speculative hands cautiously unless you can get all-in on third street. You can commit if you catch another good card by fifth street.

Triple Draw Sitngos

Triple draw is one of the most recent games to gain popularity online. Many people have learned the basics, but few have mastered this fast-paced, high-variance game whose straightforward rules and betting structure make it appear deceptively simple. Many complexities separate beginners from competent players, and competent players from experts.

The betting structure is the same as in limit hold'em. Players are dealt five cards to start with, of which they can discard as many as they like on each of three draws. The aim of the game is to make the best low, and in the most popular format of

2-7 that would be 2-3-4-5-7, since aces play high, and straights and flushes count against you. There is an A-5 version of the game, the best hand being A-2-3-4-5, but 2-7 is generally preferred, as it is more sophisticated, and it is the primary version of the game online, so we will focus on 2-7 exclusively.

Playing Pre-draw

Hand selection is your most important decision in triple draw. In early position you should stick to smooth one-card draws to an 8-6 or better, such as 2-3-4-7, 2-4-6-8 or 3-4-5-8, and 8-7 draws that can be broken into two-card draws in multi-way pots, such as 2-3-7-8 or 2-5-7-8, but played as one-card draws heads-up. You also want to play smooth seven draws that contain a deuce and two other cards (e.g., 2-3-4, 2-3-7, 2-5-7 or 2-6-7) and the smooth eight draws, which are 2-3-8, 2-4-8 and 2-5-8.

You can widen this range significantly when opening in later positions because of the advantage of both betting and drawing last. On the button, you can now open three-card draws like 2-3, 2-4, 2-5 or 2-7, bad two-card draws like 3-5-7 or bad one-card draws like 3-4-5-7 or 3-4-6-9, though in the latter cases, you will often want to fold after the first draw if you miss. In the big blind, you can defend quite wide to one bet as long as you avoid gutshots and rough draws and play 2-3, 2-4, 2-5 and 2-7, and heads-up against the small blind any two to a wheel, like 4-5 or 7-3.

You can vary from this strategy in the right circumstances, and many high-stakes players will do so significantly when they feel the time is right. For example in a weaker, more passive game you might play hands like 2-6-8, 3-4-8 and 3-5-8 from early position, and raise or defend slightly more liberally in late position and in the big blind against a weak player if you can make up for it later. Some players will even break conventional rules and call drawing three in position if a weak player raises and they have a hand like 2-7 in the small blind. Dead cards should be a consideration in pre-draw strategy, and while raising a drawing three is a vulnerable strategy outside of the button if you have dead cards in your hand like 2-2-7-7-x, you can again push the boundaries and raise in the cutoff.

The more interesting pre-draw decisions usually come in response to the actions of those in front of you. When a player raises in early position, the traditional advice has been to re-raise with strong one- or two-card draws to isolate and chop up the blinds' money. However cold-calling when you have only a two-card draw is now generally considered optimal, since when broken down, an early-position range of hands will contain a surprisingly high percentage of one-card draws and pat hands.

Another good reason to flat-call here is that when you have a smooth hand like 2-3-7 on the button that will often make a near-nut hand, you want to let players in behind you with rougher, weaker draws that will make second-best hands so that you can win a lot of bets on future streets. However you may still re-raise hands like this from the button against the cutoff, or from the small blind against the button, because their ranges are weaker, and in the latter case you would prefer to not be in the worst position in a three-handed pot.

One of the problems with sometimes calling and sometimes raising is a lack of balance. Be careful to play similar groups of hands the same way and not based on their strength. Therefore, usually cold-calling with strong two-cards draws to early-position raises (and re-raises), and re-raising or capping with one-card draws makes it difficult for opponents to guess your hand strength. This will make weak hands easier to play on later streets, present some snowing opportunities when your opponent is drawing two or bricks the first couple or draws and you have a weaker one-card draw, and make sure you get paid off with big hands.

Position is crucial in triple draw. Opponents will gain information from both your betting and drawing actions, and therefore you must play very cautiously when out of position with marginal hands. For example, in early position you should usually fold rough one-card draws that cannot break, such as 3-5-7-8 or 4-5-6-9, as the reverse implied odds are massive. You will either win the blinds and move on to the next hand or face smoother hands from out of position when some of the deuces you need are already taken. In late position however, this would be a fine hand to raise with, as you can control the pot. You can even play gutshot draws like 3-4-6-7; if you don't hit a 2, 8 or 9 straight away, you can simply snow.

Weak pat hands present a similar problem. A pat 8-7 or better is usually playable and shouldn't be broken, since you will rarely have the correct odds to draw and improve, and you will be better off folding if you are sure you are beat (unless you have a hand like 2-3-6-7-8). However, pat nines like 2-3-4-5-9 are often better off drawing to 2-3-4-5 than keeping the 9, as you will usually make a 9 or better by the end of the hand anyway and have better implied odds as opposed to reverse-implied odds. Rough nines are even more vulnerable, as they are often completely unbreakable, like 3-4-5-6-9, and so should be played in late position or at tight tables only where you can re-raise to get heads-up or steal the blinds. Similarly, against players who often raise and stand pat in late position, remember that a large part of their range is weaker hands, and that you can draw more liberally against them.

Pre-draw decisions in triple draw set the stage for the rest of the hand and dramatically impact the overall variance and number of tough decisions that you will face in the game, since once you enter a pot, you will often be drawing again, and usually a third time. Unless you have good later-street skills, good hand selection is essential, and if you are not confident in your game, you are advised to stick to the basic tight principles outlined above. If you are a more seasoned player or find yourself against particularly weak opposition, then you should definitely look to maximize your return by making some creative plays and pushing the boundaries a little to get in more pots with weak players.

The Middle Rounds

After the first draw, your decisions are usually quite easy if you have drawn smooth. You will usually want to call and draw again if you don't improve, unless your hand was very weak and rough or you were drawing three. The bet size after the first draw is the same as before the draw, and if, as often occurs, the pot is raised and re-raised pre-draw, you will be getting odds to call unless the pot is small, you face multiple bets or you have a very weak hand.

You should almost always bet if you were ahead in the previous draw. Hence, you should act based on the information you've gained from the first round of draws (if there are two players drawing the least number of cards, the last one usually bets to charge the other players, and if the draw is even, then whoever improves usually just bets). When you improve to drawing less cards than the player leading the draw, you can automatically check-raise most of the time, although you should not usually bet or check-raise when drawing the same number of cards, since your hand is never that much of a favorite and may lag behind if your opponent improves.

In terms of the cards you want to improve your hand, you still want to be drawing fairly smooth most of the time and trying to make sevens and eights, since there are two draws to come after this one, unless the situation is unusual like when you have raised with a rough nine draw such as 4-5-6-9 and hit, or have made a nine against a player drawing three when you are heads-up. Assuming your draw was fairly smooth to start with, this will make your decisions pretty straightforward, since you can just keep any cards that improve you to an eight-draw or better, or to a good three-card hand if you started out with 2-3, 2-4, 2-5 or 2-7.

If you make a pat hand, you should put in multiple bets until it becomes clear that another player might be pat with a better hand, in which case you might consider breaking a weak 8-7 with a good draw beneath it, like 2-3-6-7-8, or calling down with a weaker 8-6 like 2-4-5-6-8. With stronger hands, you will usually want to see multiple bets go in on future streets too before you slow down, and you should consider how many cards your opponents have drawn before going pat, to help determine their possible hand strength.

After the second draw the bets double, so you now have to decide how to continue. You should generally fold if you have not improved to at least a one-card draw (though in some circumstances you might draw two if the pot is big, or snow) and you will usually need to fold even a strong one-card draw facing a bet and a raise, as you may potentially have to pay 3-4 bets in total to draw again to a small number of outs. As we have seen, the number of cards drawn on the previous round decides the player who bets first. Let this be the starting point for the action, unless the draw is even, and then you can lead out to avoid missing value.

Because of the structure of the game, the bettor at this point will usually be drawing one or pat, and so you should mainly be raising or check-raising when you are not pat yourself, as there is not enough value to raising when drawing one to knock out a weaker player, or trying to make the bettor break a weak pat hand when you are still drawing, as most one-card draws run very close in equity. However, one unusual play you can make to mix things up a bit when heads-up and both players have drawn two is to check-raise your pat hands out of position, as your opponent will often bet when checked to with a wide range, assuming you will often fold, and for balance you should also occasionally snow like this when you have missed entirely.

At this stage you can usually draw again at most one-card draws unless your opponent is already pat and the pot is small, in which case you should fold most of your rougher draws, since you will rarely be getting the correct odds, assuming your opponent mostly has sevens or eights. If your opponent was already ahead in the draw and not pat, then he will often bet and be drawing one, and so now you can draw to your rougher draws like 2-3-7-8, since he will often still be drawing and the last cards dealt will frequently determine the winner, or if pat he will often have nines or tens that you are very live against.

The Later Rounds

Hands to pat with after the second draw will depend largely on the previous drawing action, the betting and the number of players in the pot. Triple draw players learn early on that a jack is a favorite against one player drawing one and a nine is a favorite against two players drawing one. But you should be more inclined to break a jack unless the pot is large or your hand is rough, since it is close to even money and will have greater reverse implied odds.

Knowing when you can pat against draws is fairly straightforward if you follow the action carefully. For example, if you are heads-up and make a ten when both players have drawn one, then you can bet and pat if checked to, or bet first and pat automatically if not raised. Similarly, if your opponent is drawing one and you are drawing two and make a pat hand, now you have an automatic raise or check-raise, since he will always bet his one-card draws.

Heads-up, when you have both drawn previously, you should freeze your opponent with a mid-range hand like an 8-7 or 9-6 when you are in position by only calling a bet. Or check-raise and pat behind when you are a favorite, as he will then often pat a worse hand. The value gained from his not drawing is greater than if you get one extra bet but he draws. This applies mainly when both players have drawn one and your opponent bets into you, indicating a pat hand, or when the draw is 2-1 in your favor and your opponent check-raises you.

Multi-way, the same principles apply, so if your two opponents draw one and check, then you can bet and pat a nine easily. Watch for situations where you can raise a marginal pat hand to achieve multiple goals. For example, if the draw goes 1/2/2, you are second to act and you make a ten, when the first player automatically bets, you can raise and knock out the third player. You can pat if he folds and the first player calls and draws. Similarly, if you are first to act with a ten here, you can bet out and pat if one player folds and the other calls.

Things get more complicated on the last drawing round when you have a marginal made hand and are raised or check-raised. Your opponent is representing a pat hand that could be very strong and value-raising against you, or weak but a favorite over a draw and hoping to get you to break. You face a decision that is complex and likely to determine your overall success at triple draw.

When facing a raise, you should rarely break a good 8-7 and rarely pat with a ten or a smooth 9-8 that can be broken. These hands are quite far ahead and behind your opponents' raising ranges, but even then you have more decisions, such as whether you should three-bet the 8-7 for value or just call, or three-bet a bad ten and hope you can force your opponent to break a better hand. Whereas many triple draw decisions are automatic, around the third draw, a lot of levelling can take place, and this is one aspect of the game that separates good or average players from great ones.

When making decisions, you should consider as much information as possible, such as previous betting and drawing action and the history and image of you and your opponent. For example, if the second draw goes 1-2 in your favor and you make 2-3-4-8-7, then you bet and are raised, you have an automatic three-bet against most players, as they will often have a much rougher pat hand and will assume you are sometimes drawing one. Similarly, if you have a tight image or have opened in early position, this would be a good spot to re-raise with a ten and pat if your opponent just calls, in an attempt to get him to fold or break a slightly better hand, especially if you are in position and can still draw if he pats.

When the decisions are closer, you may simply have to make a judgment call or take a defensive line, so if the draw is 1/1 and you bet out with a 9-7 and are raised, you may opt to just call and pat to get to showdown cheaply and make it clear that you won't break easily. If the same thing happens with a rougher hand you can't break, like 4-5-7-8-9, you may opt to just fold against a tight player, or call and fold if your opponent pats and bets the river after you pat. These decisions are more opponent-specific, but as long as you vary your play and don't do anything too exploitable, you should fare well.

In summary, when raising on the final draw against an opponent who is expected to be pat, you generally want to polarize your raising ranges to strong value hands like a good 8-6 or better and weak made hands that can still be the favorite if your opponent breaks, like a ten. Raising something like an 8-7 or 9-6 is therefore a bad idea, since better hands will not break and may three-bet you and worse hands may break and improve, and if you are both drawing one going into the last round and are bet into, then you should simply call and freeze with such hands. Similarly if the draw was 1-2 in your favor and you were check-raised, then you would apply a similar strategy and raise with the strongest and weakest hands and call with middle-strength hands.

Playing on the final betting round is equally interesting when both players have previously drawn one, as now the hand ranges for value betting and bluffing on the river change radically. The standard advice for river play here is to bet hands as weak as a jack for value (though you might check-call with a jack out of position), bluff with high pairs or straights and bluff-catch with anything up to a pair of twos. This advice often surprises new players, but it is fairly logical from a mathematical perspective, since the last card will determine the winner of the hand so often when both players have drawn one. and the pot will be large by this point. You can modulate this strategy slightly to exploit weaker or unbalanced players based on their tendencies, for example by bluffing more than this if they fold too much or rarely bluffing a player that calls too widely.

Sitngo Strategy

Triple draw is an interesting game to play in a sitngo. It is an action-packed game in which players will often draw to the end, trying to make a hand. You should generally play solid starting hands unless you encounter very weak opponents or get a chip lead. You will face high blinds as the sitngo progresses, risking elimination in a couple of hands if they do not go your way. You can't do too much about this, since you should still always raise pre-draw and re-raise with one-card draws.

To minimize variance, you can flat-call with two-card draws and not cap one-card draws when re-raised, unless you face a very bad opponent. Even then, you will often find yourself drawing to make a hand over multiple streets and have to get lucky to survive. However, if you can control the size of the pot against tight players, you can get away from more of your weaker draws when they take very strong drawing lines like 1-pat on the first two rounds, since you will now not usually be getting the correct odds to call without a seven draw and should therefore save the big bet for another hand.

Mixed-game Sitngos

It is worth considering how games interact in formats like H.O.R.S.E. or 8-game, in which you can also find sitngos. H.O.R.S.E. is a fixed-limit rotation combining hold'em, Omaha high-low, razz, stud and stud high-low (the E is for "eight or better", another name for the game). And 8-game consists of these games plus no-limit hold'em, pot-limit Omaha and triple draw.

At the beginning of a H.O.R.S.E. sitngo, play is similar to a cash game, as you will be under virtually no blind pressure due to the fixed-limit betting. This enables you to play many hands without fear of going broke. This is generally also true of the entire first rotation of games, particularly after hold'em and Omaha high-low are out of the way, because you switch to stud games which are played with bring-ins and antes which require you to commit far fewer chips relative to your stack.

This sequencing provides an interesting twist because the next time you play hold'em, you are likely to see a bottleneck, as the size of the blinds will suddenly be enormous relative to the average stack and many players who clung on through the stud games will now struggle to survive.

In a typical H.O.R.S.E. event, you might start with 1,500 chips at the 30/60 limit (with blinds of 15/30), making it effectively impossible to get knocked out in this level. However, by level six, when hold'em comes around again, you will suddenly be playing 100/200 (with blinds of 50/100) after ending the rotation playing 80/160 eight or better stud, which only required an ante of 15 and a small bring in from one player. If you still have 1,500 chips at the start of level 11 (the third hold'em level), you will be in deep trouble going from 250/500 stud high-low with an ante of 40 to 300/600 Hold'em (with blinds of 150/300).

Some planning is clearly needed at these points to ensure that you make the jump back to hold'em or maximize your chances with a short stack. You should devise your strategy a level before, when you reach stud high-low, to ensure that you know what the blinds will be, how many big blinds you currently have in your stack, and if you are very low, where the button will start and how many chances you will therefore have to find a playable hand before you are forced to post a big percentage of your stack in the big blind.

All of this might seem elementary, but it's vital to plan your strategy for transitions between stages of a H.O.R.S.E. tournament. It can also work the other way around when you are able to hang on from Omaha high-low into razz. Your chances of rebuilding are radically transformed when moving from a game where one raise is a significant percentage of your stack and good starting hands can become useless on the flop, to one where there is no blind pressure and you can wait for good hands and cheap stealing opportunities.

An 8-game sitngo generally starts with triple draw, followed by the H.O.R.S.E. games and then no-limit hold'em and pot-limit Omaha. It consists of three distinct blocks of limit games with four betting rounds, then the stud games, and then the big-bet games. Here the most dangerous transition is from pot-limit Omaha to limit hold'em, since the blinds will be very small in the big bet games but then get much bigger quickly, and again you should make the same considerations as when coming back to limit hold'em in H.O.R.S.E. sitngos.

Chapter Five

Miscellaneous Topics

Advances in Software

There have been many advances in software since the publication of *Secrets of Sitngos*. Below we discuss the currently most useful tools for sitngo players, including a couple of old favorites for new readers and some new ones that will make your play more pleasurable and profitable.

Sit And Go End Game Tools (sngegt.com)

SNGEGT is an ICM-based program which can tell you whether pushing (or calling) or folding is more profitable in a given situation, based on the hand ranges you assign to the players involved. It is particularly effective as a training tool, and even if you are not sure what hand ranges to assign to certain players, you can just move the slider up and down to find the point at which a certain play is breakeven, and decide what to do based on whether your opponents play tighter or looser than that. SNGEGT has been so effective that PokerStars has banned the "live play" version (which lets players make calculations while playing a hand). You can download a free basic version, and one such program will be essential to your success in sitngos.

SitNGo Wizard (sngwiz.com)

This program is similar to Sit And Go End Game Tools. The interface is slightly more complex, and it has a few more options than SNGEGT, which can be useful for evaluating non-standard sitngos. SitNGo Wizard can calculate situations involving multiple all-ins, and it allows you to edit the parameters for payout structures. It includes a future play simulator, which helps you make decisions in spots where ICM might be unreliable (as it does not account for blind positions) such as how to play correctly when under the gun with a very short stack, or when the blinds are very high on the bubble. A free 30-day trial is available, so you should at least give it a try.

Table Ninja (tableninja.com)

A utility for PokerStars, Table Ninja offers hotkeys, shortcuts, pot betting functions and other capabilities that will dramatically improve your online playing experience, especially if you play many tables at once or suffer from play-related injuries such as RSI. You can register for tournaments with one click. It can deal with pop-ups and closing tables, and can even auto-register you. During games, it will allow you to automate your bet sizes to predetermined amounts or percentages, create a hotkey to automatically go all-in and ensure that you never miss hands or games by automatically clicking the time bank and sitting you back if you time out. In short, it will save you vast amounts of clicks and distractions. There is a free 30-day trial.

Tourney Manager (tourneymanager.net)

Tourney Manager tracks your results based on money or buy-ins won vs. games played, and calculates other statistics, such as your finish positions and return on investment. It can be used for sitngos, multi-table sitngos and multi-table tournaments, and is a useful way to gather all of your statistics in one place.

Hold'em Manager (holdemmanager.com)

Hold'em Manager is a play-tracking product that has quickly become the industry standard and eclipsed Poker Tracker in the eyes of many top players. It tracks standard statistics for opponents, such as how often they put money in the pot (VP$IP) and how often they open-raise (PFR), and can track most other statistics that you might find valuable, and graph your results and EV. If you are remotely interested in statistics and want to keep track of your own numbers or those of your opponents, this is the program to get.

Poker Training Sites

Online training sites have become much more popular in the last few years. There are many sites of varying quality. Below we discuss the biggest and best. Whether your interest is in no-limit sitngos, cash games or mixed games, they are well worth checking out.

CardRunners (cardrunners.com)

Primary instructors:	Brian Townsend, Brian Hastings, Mike Schneider, Phil Shaw
Approx. videos to date:	2,000
Approx. sitngo videos:	200
Approx. releases per week:	10-12
Games covered:	Most games/formats
Subscription details:	$99.99 sign-up fee, $27.99 per month
Free trial:	No
DRM:	Yes

One of the oldest sites and the current market leader both in the number of videos available and the quality of instructors, CardRunners offers videos covering most games and formats from established online legends (who have recently been made Full Tilt Pros) and a strong list of guest pros. Begun as a bedroom business by Taylor "Green Plastic" Caby and Andrew "Muddywater" Wiggins in 2005, it has grown out of all proportion, signing Brian Townsend and moving to a schedule of daily videos in early 2007. They have recently responded to competition from other sites, strengthening their mid-stakes no-limit pro base and moving into a more planned and series-oriented delivery of content. Therefore, although not cheap, a membership to CardRunners is an essential purchase for any serious or aspiring poker player and is guaranteed to pay for itself many times over.

DeucesCracked (deucescracked.com)

Primary instructors:	Krantz, Foxwoods Fiend, Ansky, Vanessa Selbst, Joe Tall, Death Donkey
Approx. videos to date:	1,500
Approx. sitngo videos:	50
Approx. releases per week:	10-12
Games covered:	Most games/formats
Subscription details:	No sign-up fee, $29 per month (discounts for longer)
Free trial:	Seven-day free trial (unlimited downloads)
DRM:	No

Created from the ashes of the Threebet.net and old DeucesCracked coaching sites by a group of prominent high-stakes no-limit and mixed-game players, DeucesCracked represents the main threat to CardRunners both in terms of instructional quality and volume. Launched at the beginning of 2008 on the back of six months of detailed planning, the site quickly built a following on the basis of high-quality videos and a less restrictive content-management policy than other sites, which enables anyone to sign-up for a free trial and download as many videos as they like to watch whenever they want, without having to pay a cent. They have also tried to up the ante in terms of presentation, emphasizing entertainment value by producing content in "seasons", with multi-week series and amusing introductions. The main draw, however, remains the quality of the instruction and the now considerable library of past videos, all of which can be accessed for little or no outlay.

PokerXFactor (pokerxfactor.com)

Primary instructors:	Sheets, JohnnyBax, Rizen, BelowAbove
Approx. videos to date:	1,250
Approx. sitngo videos:	100
Approx. releases per week:	7
Games covered:	Mainly NLH tournaments and sitngos
Subscription details:	$119.95 sign-up fee, $24.95 per month
Free trial:	No
DRM:	Yes

PokerXFactor is one of the oldest sites, featuring a considerable library with well-known old-school tournament and sitngo players like Eric "Sheets" Haber and Cliff "JohnnyBax" Josephy. It is the only large site to focus almost exclusively on tournament play, with many videos of final-table play and deep runs in major tournaments. Players wanting a wider education are likely to be put off by this fact and the sign-up fee, which is the largest of any training site currently in operation.

LeggoPoker (leggopoker.com)

Primary instructors:	AE Jones, Apathy, Bobbofitos, Sauce123, Straate
Approx. number of videos:	750
Approx. sitngo videos:	None
Approx. releases per week:	4-5
Games covered:	Mainly NLHE Cash (with some PLO and MTT content)
Subscription details:	$100 sign-up fee then $30 per month (or flat rate for longer)
Free trial:	No
DRM:	Yes

LeggoPoker was created in 2007 based on the experience and vision of Greg "Mynmizgreg" Brooks and a few experienced poker coaches like Rob "BobboFitos" Eckstut, and has shot to prominence by signing some of the best young and upcoming NLHE cash players, such as Aaron Jones, Ben "Sauce123" Sulsky and Ben Straate. It has always been and remains a site dedicated to no-limit hold'em cash-game instruction, but this focus has widened recently to include some MTT videos from Peter "Apathy" Jetten and Clayton Newman, as well as PLO content. But the main attraction comes from the mix of established and capable NLHE cash players and new raw talent, and for any serious players intent on staying on top of the current games, it would be a worthwhile addition at minimal cost.

Chapter Six

Rakeback and Reward Programs

As correct sitngo strategy has become more widely known, the basic return on investment that even the best players can expect has declined. In response, players can select games more carefully, play on less popular sites, switch to lesser known formats or look for sites that have tried to compensate for this through strong rakeback and reward programs.

We will consider the options available in this last regard, beginning with rakeback comparisons and moving on to analysis of additional benefits. The best of these can be found at PokerStars in the form of their VIP Club, which at the highest levels, Supernova and Supernova Elite, offers players a far better deal than any other site. We will also look at their Battle of the Planets weekly leaderboards, where players win prizes based on their high scores.

Rakeback

One important subject for sitngo players is rakeback, which is the percentage of the rake that poker sites are willing to give back to their players as bonuses or rewards. Each site offers a different percentage, and some, such as PokerStars, have VIP schemes instead, which reward you based on your volume of play. Wherever you play, rakeback is essential to maximizing your profit.

On Full Tilt Poker you can get 27-percent rakeback, so you will receive 27 cents back on every $1 you pay in tournament fees. If you are a beginner playing 100 $11 + 1 games per month, you will rake $100 and get back $27 in that period, or $324 per year. A professional high-stakes player might play 500 games a month with an average fee of $20, meaning an enormous $2,700 in rakeback per month, or $32,400 per year.

If your return on investment is ten percent in a low- to mid-stakes game or five percent in a high-stakes game, rakeback will be a significant proportion of your earnings. In an $11+1 game, a ten-percent ROI would be $1.20, of which 27 cents might be rakeback. Without rakeback, you would make only 93 cents per game for a 7.75-percent ROI. Similarly, in a $300+20 game, a 5-percent ROI would be $16, of which $5.40 would be rakeback, without which your ROI would drop to 3.3 percent.

Rakeback clearly becomes more important at higher stakes. This is also increasingly the case as the standard of play in sitngos improves, as rakeback can turn a small loser into a modest winner. Whatever your level of play, you should take advantage of rakeback, since it is essentially free money.

You can sign up for rakeback at http://rakeupdate.com/signup/secretsofsitngos by opening a new poker-site account through one of the links with the relevant bonus code, then entering your account information in the adjacent boxes so that you can be identified by the rakeback administrators. You will be able to login using the details sent to your email account, and you can check how much rakeback you have accumulated. This figure is updated daily. Cashouts are normally processed within 24 hours and can be accessed by clicking the link below your balance and choosing from a variety of payment options, including Neteller, Money Bookers, Full Tilt Poker and Cake Poker.

Rakeback rates vary between sites, with Full Tilt Poker offering 27 percent; Bodog, Absolute Poker, Ultimate Bet, PKR, Eurolinx, Aced, NQIQ, InterPoker and Betfair offering 30 percent; and Cake Poker offering 33 percent. Sites will usually offer a bonus on your first deposit, which will be gradually paid as you accumulate rake. For example, Full Tilt Poker offers a 100-percent match bonus up to $600, meaning that if you deposit $600 or less, you can earn that much in bonuses by playing there, and smaller sites may even make bonus offers of greater than 100 percent, or for amounts up to $1,500. Wherever you play, always check the terms and conditions to see how much you need to play and in what period you must claim back this amount, since the small print can vary significantly between sites.

The biggest sites for sitngos are Full Tilt Poker, PokerStars and Cake Poker, although you may find weaker opposition on smaller sites like PRK, Betfair, Bodog and Interpoker (though there will also be less action). You may also sign up for Absolute Poker and Ultimate Bet at the above link, but players should be more cautious about playing at these sites because of a history of problems with game integrity, security and management. Experiment with different sites to find ones that suit you best in terms of standard of opposition, rakeback deals, frequency of games, security and customer service.

Wherever you play, if you hope to make serious money out of sitngos, or even if you just play a few each week, remember that rakeback is essential to maximizing your profit. Therefore if you intend to open a new account at a poker site, simply go to http://rakeupdate.com/signup/secretsofsitngos first and sign up there, and you will be able to save hundreds or even thousands of dollars over the course of your sitngo career.

PokerStars VIP Club

The best value for high-volume players is the PokerStars VIP Club, and for very dedicated players, Supernova Elite Status, which can pay close to 100-percent rakeback when bonuses, rewards and leaderboard prizes are taken into account. In its first three years, PokerStars required players to rake $200,000 to achieve this in tournament fees, equivalent to one million VIP Player Points (VPPs) at a rate of 5 VPPs per $1 raked. In 2010 the situation improved significantly, with the VPP rate increasing to 5.5 VPPs per $1 raked, reducing the overall amount of rake required to $181,818.18.

Their previous system of bonuses being awarded along the way has also improved in 2010 to benefit players who play less or at lower stakes, with the introduction of Stellar Rewards and the restructuring of the milestone bonuses for the following amounts:

Yearly	Stellar Reward[6]
750	$10
1,500	$10
2,250	$10
3,000	$10
4,000	$10
5,000	$50
10,000	$50
15,000	$50
20,000	$50
25,000	$50
30,000	$50
35,000	$50
40,000	$50
45,000	$50
50,000	$100
60,000	$100
70,000	$100
80,000	$100
90,000	$100
Total	$1,000

Yearly	Milestone Bonus[7]
100k	$1,000
200k	$3,400
300k	$3,600
400k	$3,800
500k	$4,000
600k	$4,400
700k	$4,600
800k	$5,000

In addition to these bonuses, players also receive FPPs per dollar raked, depending on their VIP status.

6 Stellar Rewards cost 1 Frequent Player Point (FPP) each to redeem, which has little change to their overall value.

[7] Milestone bonuses cost 50,000 FPPs each to redeem, which decreases their listed value by $800.

MONTHLY VIP LEVELS		
VIP Level	**VPPs Required**	**FPP Multiplier**
Bronze Star	None	N/A
Silver Star	750	50% (1.5 FPPs per VPP)
Gold Star	3,000	100% (2 FPPs per VPP)
Platinum Star	7,500	150% (2.5 FPPs per VPP)

YEARLY VIP LEVELS		
VIP Level	**VPPs Required**	**FPP Multiplier**
Supernova	100,000	250% (3.5 FPPs per VPP)
Supernova Elite	1,000,000	400% (5 FPPs per VPP)

A player who starts the year as Supernova from the previous year will earn a total of 3.5 million FPPs in a year if he achieves Supernova Elite, and a player who is already Supernova Elite from the previous year will earn five million FPPs. These can be converted on the site into bonuses of $4,000 for 250,000 FPPs ($0.016 per FPP) and act as the equivalent of rakeback on other sites. Supernova players are also eligible to enter freeroll tournaments such as the quarterly $1 million VIP events.

In addition, Supernova Elite players receive significant rewards when hitting the million-VPP mark, consisting of:

♠   A $5,200 seat to the WCOOP main event

♠   Two packages to major live events such as the WSOP Main Event, EPT Monte Carlo or PokerStars Caribbean Adventure, or one package and $10,000 cash.

Because of the variable nature of the rewards and bonuses available, the overall value of Supernova Elite can change significantly, however the following will provide a rough guide.

Item	Max Cash Value
Milestone Bonuses	$30,800
Two Major Tournaments[8]	$18,000 - $30,400
WCOOP Main Event	$5,200
FPPs[9]	$48,700 - $74,400
Total[10]	$102,700 - $135,800

Taking all of the above into account, we can therefore construct the following rakeback values for various levels of the PokerStars VIP club from Supernova up to Supernova Elite.

In this table we assume players start out as Supernova VIPs from the previous year and receive 3.5 FPPs per VPP all year, then convert them into $4,000 bonuses and take the highest value packages on reaching Supernova Elite. Note that 50,000 VPPs have been subtracted for each milestone bonus reached.

---

[8] The first figure assumes cash and AAPT Sydney, the second PCA and EPT Monte Carlo, and both are based on the cost of packages in previous years.

[9] FPP value assumes $0.016 per FPP (i.e. taking the $4,000 bonus for every 250,000 VPPs), with the lower figure being a player starting at Bronze Star and the higher one starting at Supernova Elite, having achieved it the previous year.

[10] Freerolls, leaderboards and other promotions will add to this number and further increase the value of Supernova Elite status. For example, the quarterly million-dollar freeroll for Supernova or higher players is currently worth around $150-200 per player, and there are occasional special events or accommodation upgrades for Supernova Elite players.

VPP	Rake	FPP	FPP in $	Bonuses	Total	RB%
100k	18,181	300k	4,800	2,000	6,800	37.4
200k	36,363	600k	9,600	5,400	15,000	41.25
300k	54,545	900k	14,400	9,000	23,400	42.9
400k	72,727	1.2m	19,200	12,800	32,000	44
500k	90,909	1.5m	24,000	16,800	40,800	44.88
600k	109,091	1.8m	28,800	21,200	50,000	45.83
700k	127,272	2.1m	33,600	25,800	59,400	46.67
800k	145,454	2.4m	38,400	30,800	69,200	47.58
1m	181,818	3.1m	49,600	66,400	116,000	63.8

Overall therefore, whatever level of play you achieve, you are likely to see the best rakeback offer on PokerStars, although you should still consider whether you can find softer games elsewhere that will compensate for lower rakeback.

Should I go for Supernova Elite?

Supernova Elite is certainly the best deal in terms of rakeback and rewards without being sponsored by a poker site, but it is also requires massive commitment that even many full-time players will struggle to meet. However, if you are going to try to reach it, sitngos are definitely the best option, since you can put in a high volume while earning a lot of VPPs. Many players have reached it playing relatively low stakes.

You will need to rake $181,818 in a calendar year, which translates to $15,151.50 per month, $3,496.50 per week or $498.13 per day. It's therefore worth checking your records to see how close you are to these numbers and whether you are prepared to put in the extra hours, move up in stakes and be less selective about games to make a run at it toward the end of the year.

It's simple to translate this into a number of games required, and this will illustrate the commitment needed for all but the highest-stakes players. Note that because of game volume, it will be hard to achieve an average rake of over $20 per game, since even players in $200+ games will play far more $200 and $300 games that at any other level.

Average buy-in	Games required	Approx. games per day
$315	9,091	25
$210	12,121	33
$105	20,202	55
$55	36,364	100
$23	90,909	249

At the $100 level, the prospects of reaching Supernova Elite drop off significantly due to the volume required, but for high buy-in players it should be achievable with only a few hours play per day, and for mid-stakes players with some dedication, it is still achievable. You will have to decide if you are prepared to make the commitment, whether you have the bankroll to survive the swings and if you can put in the time at the end of the year if necessary to get there. Those prepared to make the commitment can realize a virtually guaranteed and regular six-figure income for relatively little risk.

Battle of the Planets Leaderboards

In addition to the VIP club, sitngo players also enjoy the prospect of considerable leaderboard bonuses on PokerStars. Games are split into eight divisions. The top-scoring players in each division win bonuses on a weekly basis. Basically, for each division there is a Low Orbit where the best score over a block of 20 games is recorded up to a total of five blocks or 100 games, and for the High Orbit scores over blocks of 100 games are recorded with no upper limit.

Points are awarded based on finish position and number of entries, so in one-table games. 10 points are available per entry, and paid to the players who win prize money based on the payout structure. So in a ten-player game, there are 100 points distributed 50/30/20 to the top three, whereas in a six-max game there are 60 points distributed 39/21. Fewer points are awarded in multi-table games, since players winning a couple of these could easily eclipse those playing single-table games only. The divisions and prize pools are as follows.

Sit & Go Buy-in	Division Name	Low Orbit Leaderboard Prize Pool	High Orbit Leaderboard Prize Pool	Total Division Prize Pool
$1-$2.99	Mercury	$1,500	$1,500	$3,000
$3-$4.99	Mars	$2,000	$2,000	$4,000
$5-$9.99	Venus	$2,500	$2,500	$5,000
$10-$19.99	Earth	$3,000	$3,000	$6,000
$20-$49.99	Neptune	$3,500	$3,500	$7,000
$50-$99.99	Uranus	$4,000	$4,000	$8,000
$100-$299.99	Saturn	$4,500	$4,500	$9,000
$300+	Jupiter	$5,000	$5,000	$10,000

The higher the stakes played, the more prize money is on offer, and the higher the individual prizes; less people are paid per division because there are likely to be fewer contenders. Whereas 100 players in the Mercury division are paid $5-$150, in the Jupiter division only five are paid, each receiving $500-$1,500. Players competing in the highest-value games for $100 or more can expect to receive significant income from the leaderboards, since the prizes are high and the player pools small, and in the Jupiter division, it is rare to see more than 10 players even play 100 games in a week, making those who do very likely to receive a prize. For high-stakes and high-volume players, the leaderboards combined with Supernova Elite status can come close to providing 100-percent rakeback.

Leaderboard Strategy

Leaderboard prizes can contribute considerably to a sitngo player's income. The best way to maximize your earnings from these prizes is to play 100 games in at least two of the divisions that match your standard buy-ins, so that you get the maximum number of shots at the low orbit and also have a score for the high orbit. A low-stakes player might play games with buy-ins of $1-$5, a mid-stakes player may just play $60 and $115 games and a high-stakes player may just play $225 and $335 games.

It will be hard to win prizes frequently at the lower stakes, but at the mid- and especially high-stakes games, the player pools are much smaller and the average scores are much lower. Players will therefore regularly be able to cash for the leaderboard and should keep and eye on their scores in case it might be more profitable to focus on some soft or lower-stakes games within a division, or whether a particular division requires more attention to reach the required number of games by week's end. For example, in the Jupiter division, it can be hard to play 100 good games in a week at just the $300 level, and so players will need to consider whether it is worthwhile to play games at higher stakes or with mostly regulars in order to chase a prize.

Leaderboard considerations should have minimal effect on your play in specific situations. But when you are competing for a high score, it is well worth knowing exactly what needs to be achieved and the best way to do so in the last few sitngos of a block, since leaderboard prize money increases can be significant. For example, when choosing your last few games, it may be advantageous to play just six-max or full-ring, depending on the points needed to beat another player's score, or when you are in the late stages of a game, leaderboard considerations might dictate whether you should try to cash or go for the win.

Chapter Seven

Hand Quizzes

Having now covered most aspects of modern sitngo play and the various options available to players we will conclude with a quiz section designed to test players recollections of the information presented without giving them undue pointers in the right direction that would not be available in a real game. Players should therefore try to assess the most important considerations in each example before making a decision, and then see how these align with the answers and explanations given. If you find yourself picking the wrong option it is then time to re-read the relevant sections and try to reabsorb the information there before returning to the quiz again to try and understand why that action is preferable.

Heads-up Sitngos

Heads-up: Question 1

Game: $20 heads-up sitngo

Hand: 10♠-9♠

Position: Small blind

Blinds: 15/30

Stacks:

SB	BB
1,200	1,800
YOU	

Action

You raise with 10s-9s early in a $20 sitngo to 90 with effective stacks of 1,200, and are called by your loose-aggressive opponent. The flop is 2s-9h-Qh and he checks. Do you a) check, b) bet 90 or c) bet 150?

Answer

a) check. You have a marginal hand that you would like to get to showdown, but will have problems playing if you get check-raised on this draw-heavy board. Controlling the pot is therefore a good idea, especially since there are many good turn cards for you, such as low cards, spades, nines, tens and jacks, and your opponent will often try to bluff the turn.

Heads-up: Question 2

Game: $10 heads-up sitngo

Hand: J♥-J♣

Position: Big blind

Blinds: 20/40

Stacks:

SB	BB
1,500	1,500
	YOU

Action

Your wild, loose opponent opens to 120 and you re-raise to 360 with J-J and 1,500 chips early in a $10 game. He calls and the flop comes Qh-7c-3c. Do you a) bet 360, b) check-fold, c) check-raise all-in or d) check-call?

Answer

c) check-raise all-in. There is now 720 in the pot with 1,140 left in your stacks, so if you bet, you will usually have to call for pot odds. Your opponent is less likely to bluff-raise for this reason. Therefore, check-raising allows him to take a stab and for you to collect more chips from his bluffs—if he has spiked a queen, then too bad.

Heads-up: Question 3

Game:	$100 heads-up sitngo
Hand:	4♠-4♦
Position:	Big blind
Blinds:	50/100
Stacks:	

SB	BB
2,200	800
	YOU

Action

With 800 chips left in a $100 game and blinds of 50/100, your aggressive opponent goes all-in on the button. You have 4-4. Do you a) fold or b) call?

Answer

b) call. Although in these spots you are often flipping or dominated, your opponent will shove some hands containing twos, threes or fours that you dominate. You are getting odds of 9-to-7, so it's a snap call.

Heads-up: Question 4

Game: $215 full-ring sitngo

Players left: 2

Hand: Q♣-8♠

Position: Big blind

Blinds: 100/200

Stacks:

SB	BB
9,100	4,400
	YOU

Action

You are facing a maniac who moves all-in every hand from the small blind. You have Q-8o and 22 big blinds. Do you a) fold or b) call?

Answer

b) call. Since you are only competing for the remaining prize money, your $EV and your cEV are identical, so you simply need to consider your pot odds and your equity in the hand. Q-8o is almost 54 percent against a random hand and you are calling 4,200 to win 4,600, so you have an easy call.

Heads-up: Question 5

Game: $520 full-ring sitngo

Players left: 2

Hand: J♥-3♥

Position: Small blind

Blinds: 300/600

Stacks:

SB	BB
6,100	7,400
YOU	

Action

You are dealt J-3s in the small blind with 6,100 chips. You face a
tough sitngo pro in the big blind. Do you a) fold, b) call, c) raise to
1,800 or d) move all-in?

Answer

d) move all-in. J-3s has a maximum pushing value of 10.6 big blinds
and you have less than this, so you should move all-in. This will surprise many players, however the suited nature of your hand is
enough to make it worth playing (J-3o is only worth pushing with five
big blinds or less). Your hand is roughly equivalent in value to a hand
like 9-7o or Q-7o.

Heads-up: Question 6

Game: $520 full-ring sitngo

Players left: 2

Hand: K♣-5♦

Position: Big blind

Blinds: 300/600

Stacks:

SB	BB
7,400	6,100
	YOU

Action

Against the same opponent you are dealt Kc-5d in the big blind with 6,100 chips and blinds of 300/600. He moves all-in, covering you. Do you a) fold or b) call?

Answer

b) call. Again, this may surprise many players, however with these stack sizes an optimally-playing opponent will push with a massive range of hands, many of them worse than king-high, plus you are calling 5,500 to win 6,700. K-5o has a maximum calling value of 10.3 big blinds, and has similar value to a hand like Q-7s or J-8s.

Heads-up: Question 7

Game: $27 full-ring sitngo

Players left: 2

Hand: 2♠-2♥

Position: Big blind

Blinds: 200/400

Stacks:

SB	BB
7,500	6,000
	YOU

Action

You are playing against a very tight player heads-up and have 15 big blinds. He pushes all-in and covers you. Do you a) fold or b) call?

Answer

b) fold. Against an optimally-playing opponent, calling here with 2-2 would be barely profitable, with a maximum calling value of 15.1 big blinds. You should certainly fold such a marginal hand against a player who is clearly tighter than that, as his range will be weighted toward pairs that have you crushed, and you're not getting the pot odds to compensate for this.

Heads-up: Question 8

Game: $27 full-ring sitngo

Players left: 2

Hand: 2♠-3♥

Position: Small blind

Blinds: 300/600

Stacks:

	SB	BB
	6,000	7,500
	YOU	

Action

Against the same tight player, with blinds having increased to
300/600, you are dealt 2-3o in the small blind with ten big blinds.
You believe he will call with an ace or mid-high pair. Do you a) fold, b)
call, c) raise to 1,800 or d) move all-in?

Answer

d) move all-in. If the blinds were still 200/400, then raising to 1,200
would be reasonable if it would force your opponent to fold a similar
range to an all-in, but with ten big blinds, you should usually revert
to a push-or-fold strategy. Here you can push with 100 percent of
hands if your opponent calls with 26 percent or less of his range
(2-2+, A-2+, K-9o+, K-7s+, Q-10s+, J-10s).

Heads-up: Question 9

Game: $215 full-ring sitngo

Players left: 2

Hand: J♣-2♣

Position: Small blind

Blinds: 300/600/a75

Stacks:

SB	BB
6,000	7,500
YOU	

Action

You are heads-up against an opponent who you have little information on but who hasn't made any mistakes so far. You have a stack of ten big blinds. You are dealt J-2s. Do you a) fold, b) call, c) raise to 1,800 or d) move all-in?

Answer

d) move all-in. Although J-2s has a maximum pushing value of 8.8 big blinds, it is still playable with the ante. There is 1,050 in the pot, which is roughly equivalent to 350/700 blinds, meaning that you should consider your stack to be roughly equivalent to 8.6 rather than ten big blinds.

Heads-up: Question 10

Game: $109 full-ring sitngo

Players left: 2

Hand: A♠-2♣

Position: Small blind

Blinds: 100/200

Stacks:

SB	BB
5,200	8,300
YOU	

Action

You are playing a tight-passive opponent with deep stacks and are dealt A-2o in the small blind. Do you a) fold, b) call, c) raise to 500 or d) raise all-in?

Answer

c) raise to 500. Although you are well within the maximum pushing value of 29.2 big blinds for A-2 offsuit, you are likely to accomplish your purpose against this player with a raise to 500 rather than to 5,200. He is still likely to fold the majority of the time, but you will lose considerably fewer chips when he does find a strong hand. You don't mind if this player calls your raise to 500 with a few more hands, as he will usually miss the flop and fold to your continuation bet.

Heads-up: Question 11

Game: $215 full-ring sitngo

Players left: 2

Hand: A♣-7♠

Position: Big blind

Blinds: 100/200

Stacks:

SB	BB
9,000	4,500
	YOU

Action

You have just reached the heads-up stage and face a very loose, aggressive opponent who you have no experience with at this stage of a sitngo. On the first hand, you raise from the button to 600 with Ac-7s and he goes all-in for 4,500, making it 3,900 to you to win 5,100. Do you a) fold or b) call?

Answer

b) call. Since you are playing heads-up, there are no ICM considerations. You simply need to consider whether you are getting the correct pot odds to call. Calling 3,900 to win 5,100, you will need to have over 43.33-percent equity against his range to show a profit. You will have only 40.8 percent equity against any pair or any ace. However, if he will also move all-in with any face cards (K-Q, K-J and Q-J), then your equity rises to 43.6 percent, and even more if smaller suited connectors or other hands are added. Since an aggressive opponent is likely to raise with these hands, calling should be profitable.

Heads-up: Question 12

Game:	$215 full-ring sitngo
Players left:	2
Hand:	2♣-2♠
Position:	Small blind
Blinds:	100/200
Stacks:	

SB	BB
10,000	3,500
YOU	

Action

In the same game as above, you lose an all-in and find yourself down to 17.5 big blinds a few hands later. You are dealt 2-2 in the small blind. Do you a) fold, b) call, c) raise to 600 or d) move all-in?

Answer

d) move all-in. Although you have over 15 big blinds here, 2-2 will almost never be ahead if you raise and then have to call an all-in. If your opponent calls, it will be difficult to play post-flop unless you hit a set. You are well within the maximum stack size for moving all-in with 2-2 to be profitable. This is a good time to revert to an all-in strategy with a deeper stack.

Heads-up: Question 13

Game:	$5 full-ring sitngo
Players left:	2
Hand:	10♠-7♠
Position:	Small blind
Blinds:	200/400/a25
Stacks:	

SB	BB
7,000	6,500
YOU	

Action

You are heads-up with a loose-passive player who plays poorly post-flop. You are dealt 10-7s. Do you a) fold, b) call, c) raise to 1,000 or d) move all-in?

Answer

a) call. Against this player you should play small-ball to avoid risking significant amounts of chips without a hand, and try to exploit your positional and post-flop advantages. Calling here is ideal, as you will usually see a flop cheaply and can proceed from there, extracting value if you catch anything and checking it down or bluffing if not.

Heads-up: Question 14

Game: $55 full-ring sitngo

Players left: 2

Hand: A♣-2♠

Position: Big blind

Blinds: 100/200/a25

Stacks:

SB	BB
9,000	4,500
	YOU

Action

You are heads-up with 22.5 big blinds and are dealt A-2o. The loose-aggressive small blind opens to 600. Do you a) fold, b) call, c) raise to 1,800 or d) move all-in?

Answer

d) move all-in. Although you will usually be behind when called, an ace is a massive hand heads-up against a loose opener, and you need to accumulate chips whenever possible. The 850 chips in the pot will easily compensate for the times you are called and behind, and you may even be called by hands like K-Q or K-J and be ahead.

Six-max Sitngos

Six-max: Question 1

Game: $210 six-max turbo sitngo

Players left: 6

Hand: A♠-7♠

Position: Button

Blinds: 10/20

Stacks:

UTG	Hijack	Cutoff	Button	SB	BB
1,470	1,530	1,500	1,500	1,500	1,500
			YOU		

Action

Early in a six-max sitngo, you raise to 80 on the button with A-7 of spades and are called in the big blind by a loose, aggressive player. The flop comes 8♠-9♠-2♣ and you continuation-bet for 120 after your opponent checks, but he check-raises to 340. Do you a) fold, b) call or c) move all-in?

Answer

c) move all-in. You will usually lose equity when called, but in this format, you should play to accumulate chips, and it is by no means certain that your opponent will commit to the hand. Playing aggressively will allow you to increase your stack without a showdown some of the time, and it balances the times you play the same way with a very big hand like aces or kings.

Six-max: Question 2

Game: $20 six-max turbo sitngo

Players left: 3

Hand: 9-8o

Position: Button

Blinds: 100/200/a25

Stacks:

Button	SB	BB
5,000	2,000	2,000
YOU		

Action

You have 5,000 chips on the bubble of a $20 game against two stacks of 2,000 chips that are playing tight. You're dealt 9-8o and are first to act with blinds of 100/200/a25. Do you a) fold, b) raise to 500 or c) move all-in?

Answer

c) move all-in. Your opponents are unlikely to find a hand they can call with, so you will usually pick up 375 chips. You still have some equity if you are called.

Six-max: Question 3

Game: $50 six-max turbo sitngo

Players left: 3

Hand: 6-4s

Position: Small blind

Blinds: 100/200/a25

Stacks:

Button	SB	BB
6,000	1,000	2,000
	YOU	

Action

You have 1,000 chips on the bubble of a $50 game with blinds of 100/200/a25. The big stack of 6,000 folds, leaving you with 6-4s against the big blind, who has 2,000 chips. Do you a) fold or b) move all-in?

Answer

b) move all-in. You are in a desperate spot. If you fold, then the big blind will have 2,100 and you will be left with only 900. You must try to win the blinds or double through the second-place player immediately. If he calls, you still are likely to have decent equity, and winning will put you in second place.

Six-max: Question 4

Game:	$100 six-max turbo sitngo
Players left:	3
Hand:	A-4o
Position:	Button
Blinds:	75/150
Stacks:	

Button	SB	BB
2,500	1,500	5,000
YOU		

Action

On the bubble of a $100 game you have 2,500 chips against stacks of 1,500 and 5,000 in the small and big blinds, respectively. You are first to act with A-4o at 75/150. Do you a) fold, b) raise to 375, c) raise to 450 or d) move all-in?

Answer

a) fold. You are comfortably in second and should not be looking to risk chips here, particularly when the small stack may try to attack you to close the gap, or the big stack may try to leverage your desire to cash by re-raising. Fold and let the short stack make the running unless you have a hand you want to play or can sensibly move all-in.

Six-max: Question 5

Game:	$25 six-player turbo sitngo
Players left:	3
Hand:	2♠-3♣
Position:	Button
Blinds:	100/200/a25
Stacks:	

Button	SB	BB
7,000	1,000	1,000
YOU		

Action

You have a dominating chip lead in a six-max sitngo with a standard 65/35 payout structure and are up against two competent players. You are dealt 3-2o and are first to act. Do you a) fold, b) call or c) move all-in?

Answer

c) move all-in. Because of the high payout awarded to second place, this will be a +$EV move according to ICM if your opponents call with 17 percent or less of hands (3-3+, A-7o+, A-2s+, K-Qo, K-10s+), which will usually be the case against competent opposition. You should therefore be looking to move all-in every hand at this stage in order to accumulate as many chips as possible while your opponents play for second, until one of them is committed in the big blind.

Six-max: Question 6

Game:	$5 six-player turbo sitngo
Players left:	3
Hand:	A♠-Q♦
Position:	Big blind
Blinds:	100/200
Stacks:	

Button	SB	BB
5,500	1,250	2,250
		YOU

Action

You are in second place on the bubble of a $5 six-max turbo with A-Qo on the big blind. The button raises all-in and the small blind folds. Do you a) fold or b) call?

Answer

a) fold. Although calling with A-Qo is fractionally +$EV if your opponent pushes 100 percent of the time, at this level you cannot be sure he will use this strategy. Therefore, you should fold and avoid making a big error which would give the small blind a chance to advance to second place.

Two-table Sitngos

Two-table: Question 1

Game: $25 18-player turbo sitngo

Players left: 5

Hand: 9♥-9♣

Position: Small Blind

Blinds: 300/600/a50

Stacks:

UTG	Cutoff	Button	SB	BB
3,000	4,000	10,000	8,000	2,000
			YOU	

Action

On the bubble of a $25 18-man game, you are in second position overall with 8,000 chips against stacks of 10,000, 4,000, 3,000 and 2,000 to your right, at the 300/600/a50 level. You are on the small blind with 9-9 and everyone folds to the big stack, who moves all-in. Do you a) fold or b) call?

Answer

a) fold. You have a pretty good shot at second place without doing much at all, due to your large stack and the larger one of the chip leader. There is little reason to risk everything here to go for an additional ten percent of the prize pool. Fold your hand and focus on sitting tight and attacking the smaller stacks when possible.

Two-table: Question 2

Game: $100 18-player turbo sitngo

Players left: 5

Hand: A♥-10♣

Position: Big blind

Blinds: 300/600/a50

Stacks:

UTG	Hijack	Cutoff	Button	SB	BB
3,000	2,000	7,000	5,000	5,500	4,500
					YOU

Action

Six-handed in a $100 18-man game, you have 4,500 chips with stacks of 5,500, 5,000, 7,000, 2,000 and 3,000 to your right. You are on the big blind with A-10o at the 300/600/a50 level. Everyone folds to the aggressive small blind with 5,500 chips, who moves all-in. Do you a) fold or b) call?

Answer

b) call. Even though there are two short stacks to your left who are about to be decimated by the blinds, you should not be thinking too much about limping into fourth. Gambling and winning will give you an excellent shot at one of the higher positions, and you are well ahead of your opponent's hand range. Winning will also give you a chip lead that you can try to build on around the bubble since the medium stacks will want to wait for the elimination of the many short stacks before getting too involved.

Two-table: Question 3

Game: $50 20-player turbo sitngo

Players left: 5

Hand: A♥-9♣

Position: Under the gun

Blinds: 300/600/a50

Stacks:

UTG	Cutoff	Button	SB	BB
6,000	6,000	6,000	6,000	6,000
YOU				

Action

You are on the bubble of a two-table sitngo with a standard 40/30/20/10 payout. You have been dealt A-9o under the gun. Do you a) fold, b) call, c) raise to 1,800 or d) move all-in?

Answer

a) fold. With several players still to act behind you and a flat payout structure, you should avoid unnecessary risks and move up the money when other players get all-in, rather that try to accumulate a dominating stack. Here your opponents would have to call with six percent or less of hands (8-8+, A-Qo+, A-10s+) for this to be profitable according to ICM. Against so many opponents, this is unlikely to be the case.

Multi-table Sitngos

Multi-table: Question 1

Game: $5 90-player sitngo

Players left: 80

Hand: 8♥-9♥

Position: Button

Blinds: 15/30

Stacks:

UTG	+1	+2	+3	Hijack	Cutoff	Button	SB	BB
1,500	1,700	1,530	1,520	1,530	1,500	1,270	1,470	1,480
						YOU		

Action

In the second level of a $5 90-player sitngo, you have 1,270 chips and have called a raise to 90 on the button with 8h-9h after two callers. The flop is Q♣-5♥-7♥, the raiser bets 180 into the 390 pot and both callers fold. Do you a) fold, b) call, c) raise to 540 or d) move all-in?

Answer

d) move all-in. There is already 570 in the pot. The raiser has made a weak bet on a slightly draw-heavy board and may fold if you jam. You have lots of outs if you are called, and you don't mind gambling early in a multi-table sitngo to try and get chips.

Multi-table: Question 2

Game: $55 45-player sitngo

Players left: 17

Hand: Q♠-9♥

Position: Hijack

Blinds: 150/300/a25

Stacks:

UTG	+1	+2	+3	Hijack	Cutoff	Button	SB	BB
2,540	4,700	3,560	1,520	7,500	1,500	3,600	4,000	3,200
				YOU				

Action

With blinds at 150/300/a25 in a $55 45-player sitngo, you are on the hijack with a 7,500 stack and Q-9o. The next stacks have 1,500, 3,600, 4,000 (SB) and 3,200 (BB). Do you a) fold, b) call, c) raise to 750 or d) move all-in?

Answer

c) raise to 750. You are in a great spot to steal, as the larger stacks are unlikely to re-steal. You can fold to their shoves, and are easily pot-committed against the shorter stack. You have lots of chips behind if you lose to the short stack, and good pot odds from the dead money.

Multi-table: Question 3

Game:	$10 45-player sitngo
Players left:	10
Hand:	A♣-3♦
Position:	Big blind
Blinds:	400/800/a75
Stacks:	

UTG	Cutoff	Button	SB	BB
6,000	7,000	3,000	12,000	8,000
				YOU

Action

You are ten-handed on two tables in a 45-player $10 sitngo where seven get paid. You are third overall, with ten big blinds. You hold A-3o in the big blind when the chip leader in the small blind moves all-in against you. Do you a) fold or b) call?

Answer

a) fold. Although you are usually ahead of his range and would be able to play on with a big stack, at this point you are likely to see the tables break quite soon and the shorter stacks eliminated quickly at the final table. You can sit back for a couple of rounds and wait for strong hands to play while moving up without risk.

Winner-take-all Sitngos

Winner-take-all: Question 1

Game: $200 Shootout tournament (first round)

Players left: 5

Hand: A♠-Q♥

Position: Button

Blinds: 30/60

Stacks:

UTG	Cutoff	Button	SB	BB
3,600	3,500	2,500	3,000	4,000
		YOU		

Action

In a $20 satellite to a $200 event, you are in the last five with A-Qo. You re-raise on the button to 500 after the cutoff raises to 150, but he re-raises all-in, leaving you calling 2,000 to win 3,075. Do you a) fold or b) call?

Answer

b) call. You only need to win 40 percent of the time to show a profit, since there are no ICM considerations in a winner-take-all sitngo. A-Q is strong enough against most ranges to show a profit. Therefore, you should be prepared to gamble and try to build a stack that will give you a chance for the win.

Multi-prize Sitngos

Multi-prize: Question 1

Game: $80 10-player satellite to $200 tournament (four prizes)

Players left: 5

Hand: J♠-J♦

Position: Big blind

Blinds: 150/300

Stacks:

UTG	Cutoff	Button	SB	BB
3,000	3,000	3,000	3,000	3,000
				YOU

Action

You are in the big blind on the bubble of a satellite to a larger online tournament with J-J. Everyone folds to the small blind, who moves all-in. Do you a) fold or b) call?

Answer

a) Fold. Although jacks are a big hand, to call here you would need to be very sure of winning, as you are essentially creating a freeroll for the other players into the main tournament. If you fold, your equity will be $153. If you call, you will either win a seat for $200 or be eliminated with nothing, meaning you need to be a 76.5-percent favorite against his range according to ICM. Jacks are 77.5-percent against a random hand, but you would have to be absolutely sure he was moving all-in every time to consider calling. Even then, you may be better off folding if other players are likely to make foolish mistakes that would benefit you on subsequent hands. Your opponent's pushing range is key here. For example, even with K-K it would still be correct to fold if he was moving all-in with 20 percent or less of hands.

Multi-prize: Question 2

Game: $80 10-player satellite to $200 tournament (four seats)

Players left: 5

Hand: A♠-A♦

Position: Button

Blinds: 200/400/a25

Stacks:

UTG	Cutoff	Button	SB	BB
3,600	3,500	4,500	3,000	400
		YOU		

Action

You are the chip leader on the bubble of a satellite to a large online tournament and the player in the big blind is all-in. The first two players limp, and you have aces on the button. Do you a) fold, b) call, c) raise to 1,200 or d) move all-in?

Answer

b) call. Although you have aces, you should play to create the best chance to eliminate the big blind, as you get no reward for the number of chips at the end of the tournament. Raising might force the other players out, giving the big blind a better chance of survival, which would in turn reduce your $EV. Therefore, your best strategy is to call and check the hand down.

Double-or-nothing Sitngos

Double-or-nothing: Question 1

Game: $5 Double-or-nothing sitngo

Players left: 10

Hand: A♠-Q♠

Position: UTG

Blinds: 10/20

Stacks:

UTG	+1	+2	+3	+4	Hijack	Cutoff	Button	SB	BB
1,500	1,500	1,500	1,500	1,500	1,500	1,500	1,500	1,500	1,500
YOU									

Action

You have A-Qs on the first hand of a $5 game. You raise in mid-position to 60 and are re-raised to 220. Do you a) fold, b) call or c) go all-in?

Answer

a) fold. You would like to see a flop with this nice hand, but it's unwise to gamble in a large pot with it in this format when you will often be able to win without taking significant risks.

Double-or-nothing: Question 2

Game: $50 Double-or-nothing sitngo

Players left: 7

Hand: Q♣-J♦

Position: Cutoff

Blinds: 25/50

Stacks:

UTG	+1	Hijack	Cutoff	Button	SB	BB
3,000	1,500	2,500	1,500	3,000	2,500	1,500
			YOU			

Action

The blinds are 25/50 in a $50 game. Three players have been elimi-
nated, resulting in two 2,500 stacks, two 3,000 stacks and three 1,500
stacks. You are one of the latter. You hold Q-Jo on the cutoff and everyone folds to you. Do you a) fold, b) raise to 150 or c) move all-in?

Answer

b) raise to 150. You need to pick up chips to stay in contention. With
the antes in play and holding position, this is a good place to start.

Double-or-nothing: Question 3

Game: $20 Double-or-nothing sitngo

Players left: 7

Hand: 4♥-5♥

Position: Small blind

Blinds: 100/200/a25

Stacks:

UTG	+1	Hijack	Cutoff	Button	SB	BB
1,500	1,000	5,000	1,500	1,900	2,500	1,600
					YOU	

Action

The blinds are 100/200/a25 in a $20 game. Seven players remain
with stacks of between 1,000 and 5,000. Everyone folds, leaving you
in the small blind with 2,500 against a loose big blind with 1,600. You
have 4-5s. Do you a) fold, b) raise to 600 or c) move all-in?

Answer

a) fold. Moving all-in would be okay against a tight, solid player, but
you have a comfortable stack and you'll be in the money with only
two more eliminations. There is no reason to risk your position in the
tournament against a loose player who calls lightly, and you are not
desperate to double up.

Double-or-nothing: Question 4

Game:	$100 Double-or-nothing sitngo
Players left:	6
Hand:	8♥-8♣
Position:	Button
Blinds:	150/300/a25
Stacks:	

UTG	Hijack	Cutoff	Button	SB	BB
4,500	2,500	1,100	3,500	1,500	1,200
			YOU		

Action

On the bubble of a $100 game you have 3,500 chips and hold 8-8. The blinds are 150/300/a25. A player moves all-in before you for 2,500. Two small stacks of 1,200 and 1,100 remain. Do you a) fold or b) call?

Answer

a) fold. You have no reason to gamble here even with a reasonable pair, and with two short stacks, the all-in player's range will likely be very strong.

Step Sitngos

Step: Question 1

Game: $7.50 Step 1 sitngo

Players left: 9

Hand: 10♣-6♣

Position: Big blind

Blinds: 10/20

Stacks:

UTG	+1	+2	+3	Hijack	Cutoff	Button	SB	BB
1,500	1,500	1,500	1,500	1,500	1,500	1,500	1,500	1,500
								YOU

Action

Early on in a Step 1, there is a min-raise to 40 and four callers. You call in the big blind with 10♣-6♣. The flop comes 7♣-8♣-4♦ and you check. The min-raiser bets 160 into the 200 pot and two players call. Do you a) fold, b) call, c) raise to 500 or d) move all-in?

Answer

d) move all-in. You have a very strong draw and want to accumulate chips early. Shoving will ensure that you either pick up what's out there already or have a chance to win a big stack when you are unlikely to be far behind.

Step: Question 2

Game: $82 Step 3 sitngo

Players left: 3

Hand: 6♥-7♥

Position: Small blind

Blinds: 200/400/a25

Stacks:

Button	SB	BB
4,500	4,500	4,500
	YOU	

Action

On the bubble of a Step 3, you are tied with two other players at 4,500 chips at the 200/400/a25 level. You hold 6-7s in the small blind. The other players are loose and bad. The button folds. Do you a) fold, b) call, c) raise to 1,200 or d) move all-in?

Answer

a) fold. You can jam here against a good player who will often fold. Against a bad one, you risk an unnecessary all-in, and even playing a smaller pot out of position is risky. Stick to jamming strong hands unless your stack gets low, and hope the other two players get into a confrontation.

Step: Question 3

Game: $700 Step 5 sitngo

Players left: 3

Hand: A♥-7♥

Position: Big blind

Blinds: 200/400/a25

Stacks:

Button	SB	BB
6,000	3,000	4,500
		YOU

Action

On the bubble of a Step 5, you are in second place with 4,500 chips against two strong sitngo players with 3,000 and 6,000. You have A-7s in the big blind, and the blinds are 200/400/a25. The big stack folds and the short stack moves all-in from the small blind Do you a) fold or b) call?

Answer

b) call. This situation is unusual, as you have one large stack and two shorter ones. Since you are in second place, the third-place player is likely to jam on you widely to keep pace. If you fold, you have about 64.5 percent of a ticket. If you call and lose, this goes down to 28.9 percent, and if you win, it goes up to 100 percent. You win or lose about 35.5 percent of a ticket either way by calling. You should call because your opponent's range is so wide.

Pot-limit Omaha Sitngos

Pot-limit Omaha: Question 1

Game: $10 Pot-limit Omaha sitngo

Players left: 9

Hand: A♥-7♥-6♣-5♣

Position: UTG + 1

Blinds: 10/20

Stacks:

UTG	+1	+2	+3	Hijack	Cutoff	Button	SB	BB
1,500	1,500	1,500	1,500	1,500	1,500	1,500	1,500	1,500
	YOU							

Action

You have A♥-7♥-6♣-5♣ in early position in a $10 PLO sitngo. Do you a) fold, b) call, c) min-raise to 40 or d) raise pot to 70?

Answer

b) call. This is a solid hand with a wrap and a nut-flush draw, but you are likely to be out of position for the whole hand and therefore want to keep the pot small, rather than raising and having to face tough decisions later, or being re-raised and having to play a big pot.

Pot-limit Omaha: Question 2

Game: $10 Pot-limit Omaha sitngo

Players left: 9

Hand: A♥-7♥-6♣-5♣

Position: UTG + 1

Blinds: 10/20

Stacks:

UTG	+1	+2	+3	Hijack	Cutoff	Button	SB	BB
1,500	1,500	1,500	1,500	1,500	1,500	1,500	1,500	1,500
	YOU							

Action

Following on from the previous question, you call, there is a pot-sized raise and three callers, including you, take the pot to 370. The flop comes 5♥-4♦-3♦. Do you a) bet half-pot, b) bet full-pot, c) check-call or d) check-raise pot?

Answer

d) check-raise pot. You have flopped the nuts, but are out of position and still vulnerable to higher straights or flushes hitting on the turn. You hope someone will bet, which will enable you to get most of your chips in the pot now.

Pot-limit Omaha: Question 3

Game: $100 Pot-limit Omaha sitngo

Players left: 4

Hand: 9♠-10♥-J♥-Q♠

Position: Big blind

Blinds: 150/300

Stacks:

UTG	Button	SB	BB
3,000	3,000	4,000	3,500
			YOU

Action

On the bubble the blinds are 150/300 in a $100 game. You have
9-T-J-Q double-suited in the big blind and a stack of 3,500. A player
with 3,000 chips raises to 900 under the gun. Do you a) fold, b) call or
c) raise all-in?

Answer

b) call. You have a great hand, but it's unlikely to have a massive edge
all-in, and your opponent is almost never folding to a re-raise. Therefore, calling and betting any decent flop for you is a much better option. You will have ensured that you have decent equity if called, and
you will have some fold equity, as your opponent will often miss the
flop and be forced to fold.

Pot-limit Omaha High-low Sitngos

Pot-limit Omaha High-low: Question 1

Game: $50 Pot limit Omaha high-low sitngo

Players left: 9

Hand: A♥-2♥-5♣-K♣

Position: Hijack

Blinds: 10/20

Stacks:

UTG	+1	+2	+3	Hijack	Cutoff	Button	SB	BB
1,500	1,500	1,500	1,500	1,500	1,500	1,500	1,500	1,500
				YOU				

Action

A solid player opens in early position in a $50 game. You have
A♥-2♥-5♣-K♣ in middle position. Do you a) fold, b) call or c) re-raise
the pot?

Answer

b) call. Your hand is strong, but if you re-raise and he re-pots, then
you will be in a bad spot. He will likely dominate you in that case with
a big pair and low draw. Just calling and seeing the flop is the ideal
way to play it.

Pot-limit Omaha High-low: Question 2

Game: $50 Pot-limit Omaha high-low sitngo

Players left: 9

Hand: A♥-2♥-5♣-K♣

Position: Hijack

Blinds: 10/20

Stacks:

UTG	+1	+2	+3	Hijack	Cutoff	Button	SB	BB
1,500	1,500	1,500	1,500	1,500	1,500	1,500	1,500	1,500
				YOU				

Action

Following on from the previous hand, you call and everyone else folds. The flop comes K♥-4♣-6♥. You both started with 1,500, and your opponent now bets 140 into the 170 pot. Do you a) fold, b) call or c) raise the pot?

Answer

c) raise the pot. Now that you have hit a big flop, you should put maximum pressure on your opponent by raising it up. He will often have to fold, and you will almost always be in good shape when the money goes in with so many outs.

Pot-limit Omaha High-low: Question 3

Game: $50 Pot-limit Omaha high-low sitngo

Players left: 9

Hand: A♥-2♣-Q♣-5♥

Position: UTG + 1

Blinds: 10/20

Stacks:

UTG	+1	+2	+3	Hijack	Cutoff	Button	SB	BB
1,500	1,500	1,500	1,500	1,500	1,500	1,500	1,500	1,500
	YOU							

Action

You raise in early position with A♥-2♣-Q♣-5♥. The flop comes 4♦-5♦-6♦ and you bet, but there is a pot-sized raise and re-raise all-in from two tight players behind you. Do you a) fold, b) call or c) re-raise?

Answer

b) fold. You likely face a nut low and a flush, and are playing for only a quarter of the pot, with the possibility that you may be counterfeited and win nothing.

Pot-limit Omaha High-low: Question 4

Game: $10 Pot-limit Omaha high-low sitngo

Players left: 4

Hand: A♥-3♠-K♥-10♦

Position: Big blind

Blinds: 150/300

Stacks:

UTG	Button	SB	BB
3,400	1,600	2,000	6,500
			YOU

Action

On the bubble with the big stack, the second-place player with 12 big blinds opens for 2.5 big blinds. You have A-3-K-10 single-suited in the big blind. Do you a) fold, b) call or c) re-raise pot?

Answer

c) re-raise pot. With a hand that has decent two-way potential, this is an easy re-raise unless your opponent is very tight. Sometimes he will fold, and even when all-in, you will usually win at least half the pot.

Limit Hold'em Sitngos

Limit Hold'em: Question 1

Game: $50 Limit hold'em sitngo

Players left: 9

Hand: 6♥-6♦

Position: UTG + 1

Limits: 20/40

Stacks:

UTG	+1	+2	+3	Hijack	Cutoff	Button	SB	BB
1,500	1,500	1,500	1,500	1,500	1,500	1,500	1,500	1,500
	YOU							

Action

You have 6-6 in early position in a limit hold'em sitngo. Do you a) fold, b) call or c) raise?

Answer

a) fold. You do not have very good implied odds in limit hold'em. Low pairs are tough to play because you will often get good odds to call down, so it's best to just fold.

Limit Hold'em: Question 2

Game: $50 Limit hold'em sitngo

Players left: 9

Hand: 6♥-6♦

Position: UTG + 1

Limits: 10/20

Stacks:

UTG	+1	+2	+3	Hijack	Cutoff	Button	SB	BB
1,500	1,500	1,500	1,500	1,500	1,500	1,500	1,500	1,500
	YOU							

Action

You open with the 6♦-6♥ and are called by the big blind, who check-raises you on a flop of Q♥-5♥-2♠. You call and the turn comes the 3♥, so you call again. The river is the K♦, and he bets again. Do you a) fold, b) call or c) raise?

Answer

a) fold. Even though you are getting great odds, your UTG open represents a very strong range, and the flush draw hit as well. Your opponent is probably not bluffing often here, and you can get away from it.

Limit Hold'em: Question 3

Game: $200 Limit hold'em sitngo

Players left: 5

Hand: 8♣-8♠

Position: Big blind

Limits: 100/200

Stacks:

UTG	Cutoff	Button	SB	BB
1,500	2,500	4,500	3,500	3,000
				YOU

Action

Everyone folds to the button, who opens. You call in the big blind. The flop comes K♦-10♥-3♦ and you check-call, then check-call again on the 7♥ turn. The river comes the 2♠ and your opponent again bets after you check. Do you a) fold, b) call or c) raise?

Answer

b) call. You have underrepresented your hand with passive play and your opponent has opened on the button with a big stack, plus all the draws missed. Therefore you should call and expect to win often enough to show a profit.

Limit Hold'em: Question 4

Game: $20 Limit hold'em sitngo

Players left: 5

Hand: A-2o

Position: UTG + 1

Limits: 100/200

Stacks:

UTG	Cutoff	Button	SB	BB
3,500	2,000	3,000	2,000	2,500
	YOU			

Action

In the later stages of a $20 limit hold'em sitngo you have ten big blinds and A-2o on the cutoff. Do you a) fold, b) call or c) raise?

Answer

a) fold. Rag aces do not play well in limit hold'em. Here you should be particularly concerned about finding good hands before you put your last chips to use.

Limit Hold'em: Question 5

Game: $200 Limit hold'em sitngo

Players left: 5

Hand: 8-9o

Position: Big blind

Limits: 100/200

Stacks:

UTG	Cutoff	Button	SB	BB
3,500	2,000	3,000	2,000	2,500
				YOU

Action

You are in the big blind with 8-9o and the cutoff opens, do you a) fold, b) call or c) re-raise?

Answer

b) call. This hand has some potential and you are getting excellent odds, so you should take a flop and see what happens.

Limit Hold'em: Question 6

Game: $200 Limit hold'em sitngo

Players left: 5

Hand: 8-9o

Position: Big blind

Limits: 100/200

Stacks:

UTG	Cutoff	Button	SB	BB
3,500	2,000	3,000	2,000	2,500
				YOU

Action

Following on from the previous hand, you call and the flop comes
Q♥-9♥-2♣. Your opponent bets when checked to. Do you a) fold, b) call
or c) raise?

Answer

c) raise. With second pair on a draw-heavy board, your opponent may
call down with as little as ace-high. You should raise and keep betting
until raised, at which point you must reevaluate your opponent and
the board and determine how to proceed.

Limit Omaha High-low Sitngos

Limit Omaha High-low: Question 1

Game: $50 Limit Omaha high-low sitngo

Players left: 9

Hand: A♥-2♣-Q♣-5♥

Position: UTG + 1

Limits: 10/20

Stacks:

UTG	+1	+2	+3	Hijack	Cutoff	Button	SB	BB
1,500	1,500	1,500	1,500	1,500	1,500	1,500	1,500	1,500
	YOU							

Action

You have A♥-2♣-Q♣-5♥ in early position. Do you a) fold, b) call or c) raise?

Answer

c) raise. This is a premium hand with two-way potential, so you want to build a pot now and try to get a chip lead.

Limit Omaha High-low: Question 2

Game: $50 Limit Omaha high-low sitngo

Players left: 9

Hand: A♥-2♣-Q♣-5♥

Position: UTG + 1

Limits: 10/20

Stacks:

UTG	+1	+2	+3	Hijack	Cutoff	Button	SB	BB
1,500	1,500	1,500	1,500	1,500	1,500	1,500	1,500	1,500
	YOU							

Action

Following on from the previous question, the flop comes 4♦-5♦-6♦.
You bet, and you are raised and re-raised. Do you a) fold, b) call or c)
re-raise?

Answer

b) call. You have flopped the nut low. You are probably sharing it with
another player, although both players could have high hands, so you
should just call down now unless you improve or are counterfeited.

Limit Omaha High-low: Question 3

Game: $25 Limit Omaha high-low sitngo

Players left: 5

Hand: 9♦-10♣-Q♠-K♦

Position: Big blind

Limits: 50/100

Stacks:

UTG	Cutoff	Button	SB	BB
2,400	2,600	3,500	2,500	2,500
				YOU

Action

There is a raise from under the gun and a caller on the button, so you call with 9♦-10♣-Q♠-K♦ in the big blind. The flop comes 2♦-5♦-7♥ and you check, then there is a bet and a call. Do you a) fold, b) call or c) raise?

Answer

a) fold. Although you have a flush draw, it is not to the nuts and there is already a low out, so you are probably chasing half the pot and could be facing an ace-high flush draw, too. Get out now while it's cheap.

Limit Omaha High-low: Question 4

Game: $100 Limit Omaha high-low sitngo

Players left: 5

Hand: A♥-2♣-3♠-6♥

Position: Under the gun

Limits: 300/600

Stacks:

UTG	Cutoff	Button	SB	BB
2,400	2,600	3,500	2,500	2,500
YOU				

Action

You have A♥-2♣-3♠-6♥ under-the-gun with eight big blinds left. The table is five-handed, and most players are quite even. Do you a) fold, b) call or c) raise?

Answer

b) call. Your stack is very short and your hand can easily miss the flop, plus you'd like to invite other players in with weaker lows that you can take advantage of post-flop when you do hit well. Just calling allows you to get away cheaply when you miss and get more chips in well when you hit against weaker hands.

Razz Sitngos

Razz: Question 1

Game:	$20 razz sitngo
Players left:	8
Hand:	(A♥-6♥)-8♣
Position:	UTG + 1
Limits:	20/40/a5
Stacks:	

Bring-in	UTG	+1	+2	+3	+4	+5	+6
1,500	1,500	1,500	1,500	1,500	1,500	1,500	1,500
K♦	Q♥	8♣	5♠	3♦	2♦	A♣	2♥
		YOU					

Action

You are second to act with (A-6)-8. Do you a) fold, b) call or c) raise?

Answer

a) fold. Your hand is weak because of the 8-up and the other dead cards, and with lots of low cards behind you, someone else will usually get involved.

Razz: Question 2

Game: $50 razz sitngo

Players left: 8

Hand: (K♣-K♥)-A♣

Position: UTG + 5

Limits: 20/40/a5

Stacks:

Bring-in	UTG	+1	+2	+3	+4	+5	+6
1,500	1,500	1,500	1,500	1,500	1,500	1,500	1,500
K♦	Q♥	8♣	5♠	3♦	2♦	A♣	2♥
						YOU	

Action

You are now in late position with (K-K)-A. Everyone folds to you with a 2 and K behind. Do you a) fold, b) call or c) raise?

Answer

c) raise. Now you have an automatic steal with only one low card behind you and should raise here every time unless the deuce is a maniac.

Razz: Question 3

Game: $50 razz sitngo

Players left: 8

Hand: (K♣-K♥)-A♣-4♥

Position: UTG + 5

Limits: 20/40/a5

Stacks:

Bring-in	UTG	+1	+2	+3	+4	+5	+6
1,500	1,500	1,500	1,500	1,500	1,500	1,500	1,500
K♦	Q♥	8♣	5♠	3♦	2♦	A♣-4♥	2♥-Q♣
						YOU	

Action

In the same hand, you raise the ace and are called by the deuce, catching a four to his queen. Do you a) check or b) bet?

Answer

b) bet. Now you have a great chance to win, as you should bet and he should fold in this small pot.

Razz: Question 4

Game: $20 razz sitngo

Players left: 8

Hand: (A♥-3♥)-2♣-4♥-K♣

Position: UTG + 1

Limits: 20/40/a5

Stacks:

Bring-in	UTG	+1	+2	+3	+4	+5	+6
1,500	1,500	1,500	1,500	1,500	1,500	1,500	1,500
K♦	Q♥	2♣-4♥-K♣	5♠	3♦-8♦-9♣	2♦	A♣	2♠
		YOU					

Action

You raise in early position with (A♥-3♥)-2♣ and are called by a three. You bet again on fourth street when you catch a four to his eight. On fifth street you have (A♥-3♥)-2♣-4♥-K♣ against 3♦-8♦-9♣ and bet again. Your opponent raises. Do you a) fold, b) call or c) re-raise?

Answer

c) re-raise. A smooth four-card hand is actually a favorite over a made nine at this point, so you should try to get extra bets in against an unaware opponent.

Razz: Question 5

Game: $20 razz sitngo

Players left: 4

Hand: (2♣-4♥)-7♣

Position: UTG + 1

Limits: 400/800/a40

Stacks:

Bring-in	UTG	+1	+2
4,500	4,500	3,000	1,500
K♦	A♥	7♣	8♥
		YOU	

Action

On the bubble, you are in second place with one short stack behind. The big stack with an ace opens to 400 when you have (2-4)-7. Do you a) fold, b) call or c) raise?

Answer

b) call. Your opponent could easily be stealing here, but with a seven up, he can play well against you and three-bet all better hands, plus if you re-raise you will have to call fourth street if you catch bad. Keeping the pot small avoids messy situations and gives you the chance to get away on fourth street or win it quickly if you catch good and he catches bad or was stealing.

Seven-card Stud Sitngos

Seven-card Stud: Question 1

Game: $50 Stud sitngo

Players left: 8

Hand: (7♠-7♥)-A♣

Position: UTG + 5

Limits: 20/40/a5

Stacks:

Bring-in	UTG	+1	+2	+3	+4	+5	+6
1,500	1,500	1,500	1,500	1,500	1,500	1,500	1,500
2♦	Q♥	8♣	5♠	9♦	3♦	A♣	4♥
						YOU	

Action

You have (7-7)-A in late position and a tight player with a nine up raises immediately before you. Your hand is live and there are two small up-cards behind you. Do you a) fold, b) call or c) re-raise?

Answer

c) re-raise. Although its possible your opponent has a pair of nines here, you will still not be in bad shape when he does, and you may force him to fold down the line if you catch scary cards or he has a worse hand. By playing aggressively, you make it very hard for him to call down the whole way, as he will be in very bad shape when you do have a pair of aces.

Seven-card Stud: Question 2

Game: $50 Stud sitngo

Players left: 8

Hand: (Q♠-J♥)-10♠-2♠

Position: UTG + 5

Limits: 20/40/a5

Stacks:

Bring-in	UTG	+1	+2	+3	+4	+5	+6
1,500	1,500	1,500	1,500	1,500	1,500	1,500	1,500
2♦	Q♥	8♣	5♠	9♦-2♥	4♦	10♠-2♠	7♥
						YOU	

Action

In the same situation, a player raises with a 9 showing in late position into mostly low cards, and you re-raise with (Q♠-J♥)-10♠. He calls, you both catch low cards and he checks to you. Do you a) bet or b) check?

Answer

a) bet. Although you have not improved, neither has he. At least you have caught a suited card, so betting may get him to fold some very weak hands or set up a future bluff. If called, you still have a lot of overcards to his suspected pair of nines.

Seven-card Stud: Question 3

Game: $50 Stud sitngo

Players left: 8

Hand: (Q♠-J♥)-10♠-2♠-K♠

Position: UTG + 5

Limits: 20/40/a5

Stacks:

Bring-in	UTG	+1	+2	+3	+4	+5	+6
1,500	1,500	1,500	1,500	1,500	1,500	1,500	1,500
2♦	Q♥	8♣	5♠	9♦-2♥-5♥	8♦	T♠-2♠-K♠	J♥
						YOU	

Action

In the same hand, he calls you. On fifth street, you catch the K♠. He catches another low card and checks to you. Do you a) bet or b) check?

Answer

a) bet. Now that you have caught a very scary card and have many outs, you should automatically bet and he should usually fold a weak pair of nines.

Seven-card Stud: Question 4

Game: $100 Stud sitngo

Players left: 8

Hand: (A♥-K♥)-9♥-Q♥-3♠-4♣-(9♠)

Position: UTG + 3

Limits: 20/40/a5

Stacks:

Bring-in	UTG	+1	+2	+3	+4	+5	+6
1,500	1,500	1,500	1,500	1,500	1,500	1,500	1,500
2♥	Q♥	8♣	5♠	9♥-Q♥-3♠-4♣	3♦	J♣-10♣-4♠-2♦	5♦
				YOU			

Action

You raised with (A♥-K♥)-9♥ and were re-raised by the J♣, who bet every street on a board of J♣-10♣-4♠-2♦. On the river, you have (A♥-K♥)-9♥-Q♥-3♠-4♣-(9♠) for a pair of nines. Do you a) fold, b) call or c) raise?

Answer

b) call. When the pot is large and there is some chance your opponent is betting a busted draw, you should usually call for one more bet.

Seven-card Stud: Question 5

Game: $50 Stud sitngo

Players left: 8

Hand: (7♠-7♣)-K♥

Position: UTG + 5

Limits: 20/40/a5

Stacks:

Bring-in	UTG	+1	+2	+3	+4	+5	+6
1,500	1,500	1,500	1,500	1,500	1,500	1,500	1,500
2♥	K♣	J♣	K♠	7♦	3♦	K♥	5♦
						YOU	

Action

A player raises early with a Jack and you find (7♠-7♣)-K♥. Looking around you see that two kings and a seven are out. Do you a) fold, b) call or c) reraise?

Answer

a) Fold. Your hand is all but dead and belongs in the muck.

Seven-card Stud: Question 6

Game: $50 Stud sitngo

Players left: 8

Hand: (A♥-3♥)-K♥

Position: UTG + 5

Limits: 20/40/a5

Stacks:

Bring-in	UTG	+1	+2	+3	+4	+5	+6
1,500	1,500	1,500	1,500	1,500	1,500	1,500	1,500
2♠	J♣	8♣	5♠	3♥	K♥	5♦	4♠
					YOU		

Action

In late position you look down at (A♥-3♥)-K♥. A solid player showing a jack raises before you and all of your cards are live except for one heart. Do you a) fold, b) call or c) reraise?

Answer

c) Reraise. You are in a perfect situation to raise again here as even though the other player will often have a jack he will also be cautious enough to fold at a later stage sometimes and you will have many ways to win anyway. Notice that here your hand plays well heads up because of the overcards to the jack.

Seven-card Stud: Question 7

Game: $50 Stud sitngo

Players left: 8

Hand: (A♣-A♥)-4♥-7♦-9♣-2♣-(5♦)

Position: UTG + 5

Limits: 20/40/a5

Stacks:

Bring-in	UTG	+1	+2	+3	+4	+5	+6
2,000	2,000	2,000	2,000	2,000	2,000	2,000	2,000
2♦	Q♥	8♣	5♠	4♥-7♦-9♣-2♣	6♦	Q♠-J♦-T♠-2♠	3♥
				YOU			

Action

On seventh street your hand is (A♣-A♥)-4♥-7♦-9♣-2♣-(5♦) and you face a bet from an aggressive player showing Q♠-J♦-T♠-2♠ who took the betting lead from fifth street onwards. There is $140 in the pot and it is $20 to you. Do you a) fold, b) call or c) raise?

Answer

b) Call. Sure, this doesn't look too good for you – the aces didn't improve and your opponent is certainly representing two pair or better. But getting over 7-to-1 against a known aggressor you can only make a small mistake by folding, whereas if you are actually winning your gain is massive, plus you let opponents know you can't be bluffed.

Stud High-low Sitngos

Stud High-low: Question 1

Game: $20 Stud high-low sitngo

Players left: 8

Hand: (A♥-2♥)-3♥

Position: UTG + 1

Limits: 20/40/a5

Stacks:

Bring-in	UTG	+1	+2	+3	+4	+5	+6
1,500	1,500	1,500	1,500	1,500	1,500	1,500	1,500
2♦	Q♣	3♥	5♠	3♦	6♦	10♣	4♠
		YOU					

Action

Early in a stud high-low sitngo, you are dealt (A♥-3♥)-2♥. The Q♣ open-raises before you. Do you a) fold, b) call or c) re-raise?

Answer

c) re-raise. Your hand is very strong against a suspected pair of queens, as it plays well and has a hidden ace to hit. Raising ties your opponent into playing a big pot and sometimes having to call down, and charges low draws behind you to play.

Stud High-low: Question 2

Game: $20 Stud high-low sitngo

Players left: 8

Hand: (A♥-2♥)-3♥-4♥

Position: UTG + 1

Limits: 20/40/a5

Stacks:

Bring-in	UTG	+1	+2	+3	+4	+5	+6
1,500	1,500	1,500	1,500	1,500	1,500	1,500	1,500
2♦	Q♣-Q♠	3♥-4♥	5♠	3♦	6♦	10♣	4♠
		YOU					

Action

Following on from the same hand, your opponent calls and you catch the 4♥ to his Q♠. He bets out. Do you a) fold, b) call or c) raise?

Answer

c) raise. Although he probably has trips, your draw is a significant favorite, as you will often make a low and have flush outs and straight outs for high. Get in as many bets as you can, both here and on fifth street, where you will still be a favorite unless he improves.

Stud High-low: Question 3

Game: $20 Stud high-low sitngo

Players left: 4

Hand: (A♥-K♠)-K♦

Position: UTG + 2

Limits: 400/800/a40

Stacks:

Bring-in	UTG	+1	+2
3,500	4,500	3,500	2,000
2♣	Q♥	8♥	K♦
			YOU

Action

You have (A♥-K♠)-K♦ and the low stack on the bubble. The eight raises into you after the queen folds. Do you a) fold, b) call or c) re-raise?

Answer

c) re-raise. Your hand is very strong and you have no reverse implied odds, as you can get all-in quite early, so just re-raising and betting fourth and fifth streets is the best option.

Stud High-low: Question 4

Game: $20 Stud high-low sitngo

Players left: 8

Hand: (7♠-2♣)-8♥

Position: UTG

Limits: 20/40/a5

Stacks:

Bring-in	UTG	+1	+2	+3	+4	+5	+6
1,500	1,500	1,500	1,500	1,500	1,500	1,500	1,500
2♥	8♥	3♥	5♠	4♦	J♦	10♣	7♦
	YOU						

Action

You find yourself first to act with (7♠-2♣)-8♥ and there are several low cards out. Do you a) fold, b) call or c) raise?

Answer

a) fold. This is the kind of hand that will get you into a multitude of trouble however you play it as although on the face it might have some appeal it will likely struggle to win either high or low but cost you a fair amount to discover this. Get out early, and remember that even a $3 call here could end up costing you a fortune down the line.

Stud High-low: Question 5

Game: $20 Stud high-low sitngo

Players left: 8

Hand: (K♥-T♣)-K♠

Position: UTG + 5

Limits: 20/40/a5

Stacks:

Bring-in	UTG	+1	+2	+3	+4	+5	+6
1,500	1,500	1,500	1,500	1,500	1,500	1,500	1,500
2♦	A♠	4♥	9♠	J♦	4♦	K♠	10♠
						YOU	

Action

You have (K♥-T♣)-K♠ in late position and a new unknown player raises in early position showing the A♠. All fold around. Do you a) fold, b) call or c) reraise?

Answer

a) fold. Generally speaking, unless you know the raiser to be extremely loose and aggressive here you are only asking for trouble in playing an obvious pair of kings, and even then you may come to grief down the line. Even if the raiser doesn't have the bullets he will likely have some kind of low draw which makes you about even money with him, and the fact that your hand is obvious gives him a huge advantage throughout and tips the balance well in his favour. This kind of hand is probably the most misplayed in Stud High-low – proceed with extreme caution!

Stud High-low: Question 6

Game: $20 Stud high-low sitngo

Players left: 8

Hand: (A♦-8♠)-A♣-A♥-K♥-K♠

Position: UTG + 3

Limits: 20/40/a5

Stacks:

Bring-in	UTG	+1	+2	+3	+4	+5	+6
2,000	2,000	2,000	2,000	2,000	2,000	2,000	2,000
2♦	9♥	8♣	J♠	A♣-A♥-K♥-K♠	Q♦	3♥-4♥-5♥-7♠	7♣
				YOU			

Action

You have (A♦-8♠)-A♣-A♥-K♥-K♠ on sixth street and your opponent shows 3♥-4♥-5♥-7♠. He bets $20 into you, do you a) fold, b) call or c) raise?

Answer

b) call. Though this is an extreme example it illustrates the perils of raising when you have nothing to gain. Your opponents certainly has the low locked up here so by raising all you do is allow him to three bet when he has or is drawing to a straight flush that would allow him to scoop you. You almost certainly have the high locked up, but remember in this game that's only half the story.

Triple-draw Sitngos

Triple-draw: Question 1

Game: $20 Triple-draw sitngo

Players left: 6

Hand: 2-5-7-x-x

Position: Button

Limits: 20/40

Stacks:

UTG	+1	Cutoff	Button	SB	BB
1,470	1,530	1,500	1,700	1,300	1,500
			YOU		

Action

Early on in a triple draw sitngo, the first player to act opens and you have 2-5-7 on the button. Do you a) fold, b) call or c) re-raise?

Answer

b) call. Although you have a strong hand, your opponent will often have a one-card draw, and you want weaker two-card draws to call behind you and make rougher hands for when you make a seven.

Triple-draw: Question 2

Game: $20 Triple-draw sitngo

Players left: 6

Hand: 3-4-5-8-x

Position: Button

Limits: 20/40

Stacks:

UTG	+1	Cutoff	Button	SB	BB
1,470	1,530	1,500	1,700	1,300	1,500
			YOU		

Action

In the same game, you now have 3-4-5-8 on the button. Do you a) fold, b) call or c) re-raise?

Answer

re-raise. You have a strong one-card draw to number 5 and while it isn't smooth, it is doing well against his range, and you don't want to let the blinds in cheaply behind to draw to better hands.

Triple-draw: Question 3

Game: $20 Triple-draw sitngo

Players left: 6

Hand: 3-4-5-7-x

Position: Cutoff

Limits: 20/40

Stacks:

UTG	+1	Cutoff	Button	SB	BB
1,470	1,530	1,500	1,700	1,300	1,500
		YOU			

Action

You raise in the cutoff with 3-4-5-7 and are re-raised by an aggressive player on the button. Do you a) fold, b) call or c) cap?

Answer

c) cap. It is absolutely vital to not call here and give away the strength of your hand, when for one more bet you can balance effectively, and your opponent will often be drawing two anyway. Capping gives you the option to snow or get away from your hand as you want later on, and you can still make a 2, 8 or 9 for a hand you can show down.

Triple-draw: Question 4

Game: $30 Triple-draw sitngo

Players left: 6

Hand: 9-8-6-5-2

Position: Cutoff

Limits: 20/40

Stacks:

UTG	+1	Cutoff	Button	SB	BB
1,470	1,530	1,500	1,700	1,300	1,500
		YOU			

Action

You make 9-8-6-5-2 after the second draw and your opponent checks when you have both previously drawn one. Do you a) check/pat, b) bet/pat, c) check/draw or d) bet/draw?

Answer

b) bet/pat. Your opponent should almost always be drawing here, and your hand is a favorite, so you should bet and stand pat, assuming he draws.

Triple-draw: Question 5

Game: $30 Triple-draw sitngo

Players left: 5

Hand: 2-4-5-7-10

Position: Under the gun

Limits: 20/40

Stacks:

UTG	Cutoff	Button	SB	BB
1,470	1,500	1,700	2,830	1,500
YOU				

Action

You are playing tight and make 2-4-5-7-10 after raising under the gun. You've drawn one twice against an opponent who draws two twice in the big blind. Before the last draw, you bet after he checks, and now he check-raises, meaning he has a pat hand. Do you a) fold, b) call/pat, b) call/break or d) raise?

Answer

d) raise. You have a good image, have raised under the gun and have drawn one twice, so your best option is to raise, hoping to get your opponent to break a better hand or fold. He will check-raise quite wide here, assuming you are often still drawing. If he caps or calls and pats, you can then abort the play and draw.